Emotional Healing with Angels

A SPIRITUAL GUIDE TO KNOWING, HEALING AND FREEING YOUR TRUE "SELF"

ANGELS AND REKHA VIDYARTHI

Order this book online at www.trafford.com/04-2507
or email orders@trafford.com

Most Trafford titles are also available at major online book retailers.

Note for Librarians: A cataloguing record for this book is available from Library and Archives Canada at www.collectionscanada.ca/amicus/index-e.html

ISBN: 978-1-4120-4699-2

www.trafford.com

North America & international
toll-free: 1 888 232 4444 (USA & Canada)
phone: 250 383 6864 • fax: 250 383 6804 • email: info@trafford.com

The United Kingdom & Europe
phone: +44 (0)1865 722 113 • local rate: 0845 230 9601
facsimile: +44 (0)1865 722 868 • email: info.uk@trafford.com

10 9

DEDICATION

To God: Thank you for being.

Acknowledgments

I WOULD LIKE TO express my deepest thanks and gratitude to:

My editor, Della Féquet. Della is a freelance editor who has a Master's degree in English Literature from Queen's University. She has been editing text for over ten years. She currently lives in Ottawa, Ontario.

This book was copy-edited by Jane Karchmar in 2003–2004. Jane has been editing and proofreading scientific papers and books for over forty years. She lives in Kingston, Ontario. My appreciation is also extended to my daughter, Shilpa Vidyarthi, who spent many hours reading, reorganizing, asking questions and editing my writing.

And, most of all, I am extremely grateful to God and the angels for gracing my life with their wisdom, teachings and guidance as this book was being written and re-written. I undertook this book to fulfill God's will through the angels and to pass on these philosophies and teachings.

Peace and Blessings.

Rekha Vidyarthi

Contents

Preface

THIS BOOK IS INTENDED as a self-help guide that provides an understanding of the human soul – the Self – by applying angelic philosophy and teachings in our daily lives. When an individual soul chooses a journey of learning about his or her Self, emotional healing begins. This journey gives a clear understanding of negative and positive choices and reveals truths about our self that clarify life's experiences, destiny and purpose.

These life experiences consist of emotional issues (including past-life emotional issues), patterns, parental "handed-down habits" and what the angels refer to as "the seven stains" of human ignorance: ego, anger, lust, attachment, greed, hatred and jealousy. Throughout our lifetimes, we may find ourselves being tested through our interactions with people at the workplace, in our families or in other daily activities. These tests reveal how deeply engrained in our consciousness these stains may be. The tests allow us to enlist angelic and divine assistance in removing these spiritual blots or impediments.

The first stain of human ignorance is referred to as the "ego". The *ego* is expressed as "me," "I," "myself," or "pride". Our egos are tested when we take sole credit for our accomplishments without recognizing God's role. *Anger*, the second stain, is easily experienced and expressed towards others but not readily accepted as being ours in the first place. *Lust* is simply a test of morals. The Self is tested regarding a*ttachment* when we lose someone or something of material value, and we discover how long it takes to accept, to let go and to heal. *Greed* is tested in many ways, one of which is honesty. For example, if a cashier gives you back too much change for your purchase, do you return it? *Hatred*, the sixth stain, is an extremely negative and judgmental state of mind; it creates anger and revenge. *Jealousy* creates competition and a desire to harm the individual triggering the feeling. Detailed explanations and analyses of these stains are addressed in Chapter 5 of this book.

For me, the essence of learning derives from looking at particularly hurtful experiences in my life and recognizing that there are lessons to be learned from these experiences. As I began my inner journey, I became aware that deep, emotional wounds – fear, loneliness, abandonment, helplessness, emptiness, a lack of faith, trust and belief in the Self, insecurity, low self-esteem and a lack of self-love – existed well within my being. As I recognized that my outer pain was merely a projection of my inner state, I realized that I must look within for answers instead of blaming others. Finding internal answers made it easier to assume responsibility for accepting, forgiving, releasing and healing these emotions so that I could free the Self.

Learning about emotional issues *is* a journey of Self-discovery. This discovery of the inner Self leads to emotional healing that lends itself to the *freedom of Self*. This healing or freedom of the Self liberates the soul from the bondage of negativity and ultimately frees us of pain and suffering. These life lessons lead to holiness and a balanced state of consciousness. In this state, the soul becomes one with the angelic consciousness and one with God; this is the highest state the soul can achieve in one lifetime. This state of consciousness is referred to as eternal bliss.

Introduction to Angelic Wisdom

Please protect, bless and cleanse this chapter. Thank you.

A MULTITUDE OF ANGELS are appointed by God as healers of the human soul. Each soul has angelic teachers that lead us to knowledge of the Self or the soul. This book is based on angelic teachings and philosophies that can help us heal issues of the heart and Self. These teachings are universal, and their basic philosophy applies to all souls. All have access to angelic teachings within the Self, but we must allow ourselves to hear, feel, accept and follow our inner feelings.

Angelic teachings begin on the physical level: within our daily lives and through our interactions with others. Incidents may occur where emotional pain and heartache are experienced. We may need to deal with an issue of anger or a re-awakening of a childhood trauma. Or we may simply be searching for answers to current problems or guidance for the day. Angels lead us towards these experiences so that we may learn. These lessons in learning depend upon individual need and the soul's chosen journey. It is important to remember there are no right or wrong choices, and hardships are merely lessons in learning.

The inner Self reaches out, but often we do not listen or sense its gentle prodding. Sometimes we linger in a wounded state where we feel sorry for ourselves and feel a sense of hopelessness. If we do not deal with our emotional issues, depression may be the high price we pay. We move on to a healing stage when we become aware and accept that everything happens in life for our emotional growth and healing in order to know our soul. Personally, I lingered long in a state of depression until one day I realized that I had to forgive myself for my self-pity and for holding on to negative energy for so long. When I asked for divine forgiveness for my inability to see the truth, I moved on and have never looked back. In other words, I accepted responsibility for my role in my pain, forgave others for their part, healed the issue, and continued onward.

Acceptance is the first, and perhaps the hardest step in the learning process. Without acceptance, there is no learning or healing. Acceptance is the balance of blame and judgment.[1] We must understand that no one is to blame for what happens in our lives. Everything that happens presents an opportunity to learn. Human ego gets in our soul's way with all its emotional actions and reactions, e.g., anger; anger often results in blame and projecting our issues onto someone or something else rather than focussing on ourselves. If we ask ourselves, "Is this truly the way I am feeling?" then it becomes our issue. The other individual merely reflects what we are feeling. Acceptance is just another step in the learning

1 In this instance, and other instances throughout this book, I use the word balance to mean *'opposite of'* as in 'opposite end of the spectrum or 'opposite end of the scale'.

process. If there is no acceptance, there is no humility; humility balances the ego.

When we react with our emotions the ego operates through judgment. These ego-based reactions can make us arrogant and ignorant. Answers come to us as a quick reaction from a superficial understanding of the question rather than more profound responses from within the heart and Self. Ego prevents us from listening to, agreeing with and accepting our inner voice.

Learning about our emotions leads us to a discovery of Self. Learning is a step toward healing, which leads us to the freedom of Self. Tests lead us to holiness and a balanced state of consciousness, which are achieved by learning. Total and absolute focus on the Self is key in learning life's lessons. This is not to be viewed as arrogance or self-centeredness, but rather as focussing on the greater Self. When we analyze everything in and about life, we ask important questions. When we do, we discover the answers reside within us. Self-exploration leads to self-awareness. Wise people live in the knowledge of this truism and in the knowledge that acceptance is vital to spiritual growth.

Angels lead us down this path of spiritual growth through our daily experiences. There are no accidents or co-incidences; all occurrences happen as the angels have scheduled in our Book of Life. These experiences become our life lessons. Destiny, fate and purpose in life depend upon individual freedom of choice. As the individual soul makes its choices, the angels provide. The angels are all-knowing. Everything is pre-written and predestined in the individual's Book of Life. The teachings are complete once we have experienced, understood and endured a lesson physically – this may be from a past-life issue or a childhood trauma. Only then can our hearts be healed so that our Self may be free. Freedom of Self sets the mind free from negative conditioning. An absolutely non-judgmental mind frees us from negative conditioning and is in communication with the soul.

In learning from God and the angels, an individual soul requires patience, tolerance, discipline, trust, faith, belief and acceptance to follow the urgings of our hearts and souls. Listen and feel deeply, have trust, faith and understanding; without these, we will not move forward. Trust yourself, your instincts, and the teachings. Feel it, know it, and act upon it. Make a decision. Decisions lead to discovery. What you will discover is a wholeness that brings about a balanced state of consciousness. In this state humans can guide others through the process of angelic healing. Humans then become examples of angels at work.

We achieve this balanced stated when we recognize that deliverance (from stains and emotional issues), success, oneness, and happiness all derive from healing the Self. Yet we have a freedom of choice, either to walk the path of balance or lose the balance. For example, every time I got angry I was told that I had lost my balance. It took me years to practice the angels' teachings and to learn my lessons. Emotional issues stood in the way of my soul knowing my Self.

Know that everything ultimately leads to a balanced state; as we walk the path of balance (wholeness) and of healing, the angels guide us. They accept us as we are (complete with faults), give us answers so that we recognize the source of our pain (usually childhood issues[2]) and then heal us. In this way, the issues do not repeat, and a change in understanding or consciousness takes place.

When we choose to walk the path of being balanced and becoming healed, the ultimate results depends upon the level of acceptance of self we have reached, and to that level we will be healed. The angels know if we have learned our lesson completely. A journey of self-growth and healing is based on faith, a desire to know the truth and improve the Self. Learning through acceptance and following the will of God, remains our choice from the beginning to the end of this journey.

The spiritual journey is a process of acceptance and learning; without learning the journey is empty. Learning about our emotional issues and healing them is a long, difficult and extremely lonely journey. When the soul is ready, the journey begins. We are given the freedom of choice to turn away from learning or from the angels. We must know that everything in life has a purpose – a purpose based in learning to know our self. Healing is not a given – it must be earned.

We are all on our own journey; every journey is different. All lessons are the same, but they are presented in different manners. Divine creativity has no limit in its ways to teach the human soul. Healing results in learning to love oneself. The purpose of healing is to become one with God and the angels. This is the soul's ultimate destiny and our means to achieve balance and wholeness.

No human soul is all-knowing; only God and the angels are omniscient. The soul, however, is provided with everything that it needs to know. No human soul can become God or an angel, but we can become one with God and the angels. We

2 If not childhood issues, these are issues that were unresolved in a past-life.

can walk the path of a balanced state – the path of a healer who the angels guide, accept and heal. Angels always provide answers for what we seek, even though we may not always recognize this. They hear our prayers, but sometimes prayers go unanswered if our intentions are unworthy, dishonourable and self-centered. If a prayer is prayed with an honest and grateful heart, pay attention to your thoughts and feelings. You will find your answer in your thoughts.

If you recognize any new awakening, give thanks in humility to God and the angels.

Thank you, angels, for providing your wisdom
and knowledge to us mortals.

Prayer

Please protect, bless and cleanse this chapter. Thank you.

PRAYER IS A VERY IMPORTANT PART of the spiritual journey. It connects us to God and the angels. Prayers are always heard by the angels but are not always answered in the manner we may expect, or we may not receive the answer we desire. We must be very precise, clear and specific in our prayer requests and must make certain that our heart's intention is pure and clean. Prayer is also used as a form of angelic teaching. Angels teach us in a collective manner whereby by teaching one soul, all souls benefit.

When you choose to follow a spiritual path, you may discover that you live in prayer; it naturally becomes part of your daily routine. When we truly understand the meaning of our hardships, as revealed through our emotional ordeals, we express thanks to God and the angels for their teachings and the lessons we have learned. Prayers become expressions of gratitude. When prayers for healing have been granted, it is very important to give thanks. When we learn lessons of humility, we give thanks and show gratitude to God and the angels.

While prayers are personal and stem from the individual heart, the following prayer is specifically designed to enlist angelic help for healing, protection, blessings, forgiveness, and cleansing for ourselves and others. This **Prayer for Healing** was given to me by the angels and consists of three main parts: protection and cleansing of the Self, protection prayer for daily activities, and cleansing for everything and all souls.[3]

1. Protection and Cleansing of the Self

Because of the constant negativity that the soul encounters on its earthly journey, prayer for protection and cleansing is very important. Just as we have positive energy in the form of the spiritual consciousness of the soul, we also have negative energy in the form of human consciousness generated from our heart. This part of the prayer gives us protection from any overpowering negativity and negative thoughts.

> *Blessed angels of God, we invite thee into our lives to provide us with Divine Light by placing a circle of protection around our soul name,*[4] *our family, friends and loved ones [*specify names*], our heart, intellect, thought-forms*[5] *and spirits, and our home and material possessions. We invoke Divine*

3 A friend and I were given this prayer over a period of two months in 1994 when we started our spiritual journey or "lessons in learning". Angelic encounters may be visual where someone gifted with inner sight, or clairvoyance, can see the angels while praying. Clairsentient persons may experience angels as a tingling, hot or cold sensation in the body.

4 The angels address or see us as a soul with a name.

5 Thought-forms, as used here, represent the forms assumed by our thoughts, whether visual or auditory, negative or positive perceptions, feelings and knowing.

intervention by binding the negative energies and powers in Cords of Divine Light where none shall escape. All are rendered powerless by the all-knowing, all-seeing Creator. Cast all negativity into infinite love and light, never to return. Fill all spaces with Divine Sacred Light. We invite the Holy Host to walk with us in the daily journeys of our lives. We ask for guidance and accept all teachings with serenity and gratitude.

The angel made sure that I clearly understood the meaning of this last sentence, otherwise I was told I should not be praying for assistance. By this it was meant that if I ask for angelic guidance then I should be willing to accept everything, everyone and every situation in my life because all people and situations occurring in my life provide opportunities for learning. As we learn, we begin the healing process and work in conjunction with the angels. When we ask for angelic protection during sleep – simply, asking them to hold our hands – we honour their presence in our daily lives.

We thank God and the angels for divine protection and blessings.

2. Protection Prayer for Daily Activities

An individual soul can modify this prayer according to his or her specific needs and journey. While I address specific angels and their tasks in Chapter Four of this book, you may notice that golden angels are invoked for this particular prayer.

We invite golden angels to provide us with a golden bubble of light singularly and collectively. Wrap us in divine white light sheets as we walk and drive through the daily journeys of our lives.[6] *Any and all negativity – known or unknown, seen or unseen – people and material forms that we encounter or touch, as well as any of the above negativity that enters our minds, our stains, issues and patterns [name them]; all our worries and concerns; all the day's work and events. Let all our lessons be automatically bubbled,*[7] *bound in cords of Divine Light. None shall escape. All are rendered powerless by the All-Knowing, All-Seeing Creator who casts out all negativity into love and light, never to return. Fill all spaces with Divine Sacred Light.*[8]

We thank the Creator and the Holy Host for divine healing and health.

3. Prayer for Cleansing

Cleansing is an extremely important part of the prayer. In this part of the prayer, we simply hand over to the angels our recently recognized lessons, our emotional issues, patterns, worries and concerns. We bubble everything and discard it by prayer. God and the angels have only pure, clean and posi-

6 The bubble of light and the circle of light are the Golden and White Divine Lights together in a form of rope that protect us from negative energy entering the bubble and our body. Everything needs to be enclosed in a Divine Light bubble so that none of the negative energy can escape as the Divine Light binds it, like a spiral rope, until the negative entity bursts into flames and is cast away.

7 The term "bubbled," which will be used a number of times in this book, refers to the process described in footnote 4.

8 This is a crucial phrase and must never be omitted.

tive energy; they cannot take anything from us unless it is cleansed. Therefore, we request the angels to cleanse everything before releasing it into the Divine Light. This process releases us from negative energies. The prayer for cleansing begins as follows:

> *We invoke the spiral fire angels of God to cleanse our heart, intellect, thought-forms and spirit. We request cleansing for our daily journey, work, issues, worries, concerns, etc. We request the angels' conscience to be our guide. We give it all to the Divine Light of the Creator and the Holy Host. We request blessing and forgiveness for all souls as we forgive ourselves for inviting* [name the incident] *through our issues and patterns in our lives.*
>
> *We thank you, God and the angels.*

A white unicorn, with spiral fire energy emerging from his horn, was shown to me. He cleansed my entire body with a gentle touch of his horn.

4. Prayer of Gratitude

The prayer of gratitude is an individualized and personal prayer, therefore it is not prescribed. We can thank God and the angels for whatever we feel grateful for in our lives. Gratitude brings humility and a humble and contrite heart will be receptive to the angels' teachings about life.

Summing-up Prayer

Please protect, cleanse, bless and forgive all. Please provide us with the understanding to accept everyone without casting judgment upon anyone. Thank you.

If we say all three parts of this prayer over water, it becomes holy water and will have healing properties.

Spiritual Growth & the Process of Spiritual Cleansing

Please protect, bless and cleanse the following chapter. Thank you.

LEARNING IS BY TRIAL and error, and experiences in learning with the angels are no different. Angelic guidance is provided as a word, a phrase, a picture in our mind or a thought-form. We have to figure out the meaning ourselves and then act upon it. When we finally get it right, confirmation is given, and the next phase of our lesson begins.

Once we make a conscious decision to follow the angels' teachings, they will commence the soul's journey according to our individual "blueprint": as it is written in the Book of Life. The Book of Life reveals all of our past, present and future lifetimes. Everything happens in accordance with angelic time, not human time.[9] My journey began with a *battle against negative* power. I enlisted the help of the angels by

9 Angelic time means when our consciousness reaches a certain level of self-acceptance or self-awareness.

beginning with a prayer for protection and received guidance and instruction. I was told that in the end the truth would win.

In this battle, I came to the conclusion that one must never underestimate negative power – it wears many disguises and practices games and trickery. I learned that one must always be aware of its existence. Ultimately this battle proved to be a test of my endurance of truth, trust and faith in prayer. The end result made me fully aware of the constant angelic presence. I had to experience and persevere through this battle because it was necessary for the growth of my soul. Chapter Four gives a detailed account of this experience with negative entities.

My active search for the truth began in 1980. I had stayed ten long years on one path, then I resumed my search. I continued to learn as much as I could and began hands-on healing in search of answers. I would later come to know that these learning processes had already been prescribed in my Book of Life. I finally arrived at angelic teaching. Prior to this, I could hear them in my thoughts telling me that it was time to move on – towards the end of my 10-year journey. It is important to note that even as a child, I heard and saw an angel in human form many times. He was always giving me advice about positive and negative choices in life, but I chose not to listen and walked away from him. At that time I thought the angel was God (I felt this way because the angel carried the essence of God). It was not important for him to tell me who he was because Hindu philosophy does not include angels. Later I knew instantly that this angel, who I had thought was God, was the Blue Angel whom I speak of in subsequent chapters. When he resumed teaching me as an adult, I recognized his voice and manner of speaking. As an adult I just did not understand who was speaking to me in my thoughts because I could not imagine that God would return to my life once again. Perhaps it does not matter to the angels what we call them: whether it be master, teacher, angel or God. Their main purpose is to teach a human soul who is willing and ready to listen and learn. I realized I had nothing to lose so I followed their advice and moved on to hands-on healing. At the end of this learning experience, I arrived at angelic teachings.

In learning with the angels, I have discovered that everything in life has a time and place; everything is part of the learning process. I was also taught that truth comes from the Self; it cannot be handed down by someone else's consciousness. Truth has to be original through our Self (from within) and reached with angelic guidance. Everyone is capable of receiving truth from within if they choose, but it is important to cleanse and purify the old consciousness in order to receive the "truth of Self" from the angels. The second step in my spiritual growth was spiritual cleansing and the following is what the angels told me about it.

The Seven Levels of Spiritual Cleansing

Physical Cleansing

Our belief systems begin on the physical plane with our parents. As we grow up, we believe in others who claim to know truth. These are beliefs that others pass on or hand down to us. While they may have value and merit in themselves, we must learn to believe in ourselves and find our own personal truth. In order to believe in myself I had to rid myself of all my material possessions connected to the different spiritual teachings I had studied such as books, tapes, pictures, etc. This is not to say they did not have value in themselves. They were vital to my learning up to this point, but I needed to begin with a clean slate so that I could continue on my path towards greater spiritual growth. On this level, lessons around my stains such as ego, anger, attachment, greed, lust, etc. were presented, tested and ultimately, released.

Emotional Cleansing

On an emotional level, we must be willing to rid ourselves of all emotional ties and attachments to spiritual paths and personalities and seek the help of the angels. We must seek out and heal whatever emotional issues we carry in our hearts. I was shown what issues I needed to release and was given this visualization:

> *First request the Angel to bubble the memory, issue or attachment. Bind it in cords of Divine Light so none shall escape. All are rendered powerless by the all-knowing and all-seeing Creator who casts out all negativity into infinet love and light never to return and fills all spaces with Divine, Sacred Light. Then request healing and cleansing by the spiral fire of the angel of God so that the heart, intellect and soul are cleansed from this memory, issue or attachment. Release it into the Divine Light of the Cre-*

ator and thank the angels for their assistance.

Intellectual Cleansing

We erase the memories of our acquired teachings with the help of the angels by using the above visualization. This is done in order to regain *our own* original thought-forms and understanding from *our own* experiences of the Self. We practice non-judgment to set our minds free from negative conditioning.

Spiritual Cleansing

Healing of Self takes place on this level of spiritual cleansing. When the Self is healed, we gain freedom of Self and find love for the Self. We validate the trust, belief, faith and loyalty in the Self and the angels' teachings. We must acknowledge the presence of the angels in every aspect of our lives instead of assuming that things happen without a reason.

Chakra Cleansing

Chakras are points of energy (light) contained within the body. Each chakra corresponds to a level of spiritual cleansing. The angels work with our chakras to heal, align and balance the energy on each level.

Metaphysical Cleansing

Confusion is worked out on the metaphysical level. When we become too intellectually involved in the interpretation of our experiences, our emotions and imagination get in the soul's way of finding true meaning, and often we are left confused. The angels work to heal and clear the intellectually-blended emotions, which brings about a balanced state and a deeper understanding of Self and God. Once we know the Self, this level is automatically avoided.

Auric Layers

Auric layers are the physical body's energy layers extended outside the body. It is the angels' work to heal and balance energy on this level.

❁ ❁ ❁

Until this point in my spiritual search, the most attention had been paid to the levels that required the least attention, and the least attention had been paid to the levels that required the most. For this reason, all the other paths I followed left me with unresolved questions and an inability to work on my Self. An understanding of the last three levels – the chakras, metaphysical and auric levels – is beyond the reach and comprehension of the human mind. Our work and attention, along with the angels' help, is required on the first four levels. Then the angels automatically heal us on the other three levels. All seven levels are involved simultaneously in healing issues of heart and Self.

We work on the first four levels by asking the angels for help, understanding and healing. We may question why things happen in life the way they do and why we go through what we do. We also ask what changes are necessary so that we may accept that we do indeed need to change; healing of Self then begins. As long as the first four levels remain out of balance, we cannot achieve our spiritual purpose.

After getting rid of most of my material possessions on spirituality, i.e., reading material, some spiritual literature still remained. I did not think it was all that important, but I was gravely mistaken. The angels knew everything. We cannot pick and choose for our own convenience; either I followed the angels' teachings or that of others! Either I should get rid of absolutely everything or keep those few notes on spirituality. The choice was mine.

I still wanted to keep those notes. The angels showed me that I was sitting in the middle of a maze and was lost. It took me two days to figure out the meaning of this symbolic representation. The maze represented the different teachings (paths) that led to different doors. I was in the middle of all of this and did not know where to go. This was enough to convince me to get rid of the spiritual literature because I did not want to be lost for the rest of my life. This was the lesson of my attachment, lack of self-trust, belief in the Self and in the angels' guidance.

I prayed a lot, asking forgiveness for my ignorance, and the angels forgave me. I made a lot of mistakes but through these mistakes, I realized I had to follow the teachings exactly the way they had been given. It took me approximately one month to complete all levels of cleansing. I was told that my search was over, and my journey had just begun. I discovered that there was still one more box containing my old spiritual books, which had been left in my basement without my knowledge. I was given a vision of the angels standing with their backs facing the box. I had no idea where this box was, but, eventually, I found it and got rid of it as well.

The angels teach each soul individually. The angels will begin the process of healing by leading the individual to discover what level of spiritual cleansing is required as written in his or her Book of Life. While I have used my own personal experiences to illustrate the process of spiritual cleansing, this is but an example of the basic reasons for cleansing and the structural process. Simply put, it is as if the angels were saying "How would you ever trust in yourself if you keep following others?"

The process and levels of spiritual cleansing is an interface of the angels' philosophy and teachings. Spiritual cleansing is a continuous process in the ongoing journey. It was a very important first step in receiving angelic instruction and guidance during my spiritual quest. I cannot pick and choose teachings from various paths (including the angels' teachings). I have to follow the angels' teachings wholly and fully or remain with the other path of my choice. The choice was mine. Freedom of choice is a privilege of free will. The individual decides.

Thank you, angels, for providing your wisdom
and knowledge to us mortals.

Angelic Encounters & the Task of Writing This Book

Please protect, bless, and cleanse the following chapter. Thank you.

ANGELS ARE BEINGS OF Divine Light created by God as an extension of God. for the freedom and salvation of human souls. It is as important to save one soul as it is to save all. As messengers of God's wisdom and intelligence for mortals, angels maintain the balance of negative energy in the universe as well as on earth. God is omniscient, omnipresent and omnipotent and angels, being an essence of God, know all, see all and are infinitely wise and powerful. They are present with us at all times whether or not we are able to perceive them. It is important to note that when angels are present, the Creator is present.

Angels are calm, composed, serene and express eternal bliss. To me their energy felt like male energy, yet the energy can be male or female. They are wise, creative and have God's unconditional love for all souls. They are also playful, joy-filled, humorous, and encouraging. Angels dance with joy when a human soul makes even one small step towards advancement in spiritual growth. An experience with God and the angels leaves one in a balanced state and evokes an uplifting feeling in the soul. The angels will allow human souls the experience of seeing them and God; when we are ready.

All souls have angels watching over them from the time they are born until the time they leave this earthly existence. Souls on any other level of existence are also guarded by angels. Angels exist within and without. In other words, the angels exist within us, outside of us, in everyone and everywhere. It is up to us to make a conscious effort to acknowledge their presence and their teachings in our daily lives.

Angels are always guiding and saving innocent souls from the apparent danger of death, harm or life-threatening situations. We acknowledge this as a miracle of God for the soul has been given another chance to live in order to complete its lessons in learning. These experiences change one's perspective entirely because angels touch us within our souls. These experiences remain with us forever.

There is no lack in Divine creativity. The angels heal, teach and save souls in many different ways. Angels can appear in any form, from human to Divine Beings of Light. These forms are taken by the angels with respect for us, to keep us in balance during the experience. When their task is completed, they simply vanish.

Angelic Encounters

There are a multitude of angels whose ultimate purpose is to heal the human soul. Angels heal souls daily; no one receives healing without angelic assistance. Angels are of varying sizes, shapes and colours (rainbow colours), yet there is no difference in their strength. All angels perform different tasks, but these tasks are interchangeable. While specific tasks may be assigned to particular angels, they share common abilities; For instance, all angels can destroy negative energy, heal, cleanse, teach and bring us closer to our God consciousness. The following are examples of some angels I have worked with and their tasks.

The Blue Angel

The Blue Angel is an angel of Justice and Truth who is a teacher, healer and messenger. The Blue Angel has complete knowledge of the dark energy and its negative entities and knowledge of how to destroy them. The dark energy and its negative entities cannot harm us while this Angel is present. The Blue Angel is also a Guardian Angel for all souls.

The White Angel

This angel writes and records each soul's journey in his or her Book of Life. The Book of Life contains the information of the past, present and future of each soul on earth and on other dimensions. The White Angel knows of our soul's intentions and the choices that we are going to make. It knows the destiny of each soul and gives us direction in life.

The White Angel with Golden Eyes

The golden light from this Angel's eyes lights the way for souls to follow their salvation and redemption.

The Golden Angel

The Golden Angel is an angel of wisdom, knowledge and prophecy. This angel knows our future and guides us by way of awakenings and instructs us on our life's mission and purpose. The Golden Angel is also the angel for healing and protection and has purifying Golden Divine Light to cleanse our heart, intellect, thought-forms and spirit.

The Pink Angel

The Pink Angel is an angel of unconditional love and peace who guides souls towards the Divine Light and fills their hearts with God's unconditional love.

The Angel of Spiral Fire

The Angel of Spiral Fire is an angel of healing and cleansing who also burns and destroys disguised negative entities. The Spiral Fire Angel, in the form of a spiral fire of Divine White Light of God, protects and heals as well. The white unicorn is a representation of this angel.

The Angel with the Divine Sword

This angel carries a sword of righteousness that is not a weapon. The sword represents honesty and integrity. It maintains a balance between positive and negative energies. The sword is filled with Divine White Light. It is cross-like, with a rounded tip, and is held in the angel's hand with its tip pointing downwards. The sword can be used to release and cleanse negative energies.

The Angel with a Hat

The Angel with a Hat is a warrior angel with its own army of angels. It carries all souls' responsibility to fight their initial battle with the negative entities. Once its task is finished, the responsibility is given back to the individual soul.

The Emerald Angel

The Emerald Angel clears confusion created in our minds by our emotional imbalances. By simply giving over our confusion to the angel through prayer, our minds will be cleared.

The Cold Chill Angel

This is an angel of confirmation and protection. When we feel a cool sensation going through our being or on a certain place on our body, this is a sign that everything is going well, and we are being protected by the angels. This could be a white, gold or blue Angel.

The Sweet-Scented Angel

This angel carries a sweet floral scent of the universe. When this angel is present and wants you to acknowledge its presence, you will smell this scent. Sometimes it smells like an essence that is a mixture of roses and lilacs. I often have this angel present while I am writing my experiences and lessons.

The Creator

I was shown the Creator as a shaft of bright, blinding, white light. Included in this vision was the throne of the all-seeing, all-knowing, living and breathing Creator, a large crown and a huge, white waterfall. When the Creator was present in my experiences, this is what I was shown. It is as we perceive.

While the beginning of this chapter gives brief descriptions of the angels I have encountered, the remainder will describe these experiences in more detail and focus on the instruction I was given. I would like to point out that at times I experienced pain like a headache or a constant pull or tug on my head. This is a common occurrence during instruction. It is an indication by the angels that we are doing something wrong, or we have come in contact with negative energy. Correcting our mistakes and doing the Protection Prayer (all three parts) usually clears this up.

Being Tasked with the Writing of This Book

The angels chose to teach another lady (who for reasons of privacy will remain unnamed) and myself so I could write their teachings in a book on their behalf. In October 1994, they brought the two of us together. The first time I met this lady was when she came to see me for a spiritual healing session. The angels healed her of the physical pain she was experiencing at that time. We instantly became friends. The angels arranged to bring both of us together and while neither of us knew what would happen, we listened, learned and followed the angelic instructions.

Often we spoke on the phone, and she would tell me about things that were bothering her. We would analyze the issue to find the root of the problem, and unfailingly the answers were found in her childhood experiences. The angels would then heal her, and I soon discovered that I was being healed of my issues in the same manner.

From the very first healing, this lady began to see sparkles of light in a rainbow of colours. I told her that these were the angels healing and cleansing her mind, body and soul. During one of our telephone conversations, she asked why she could not see the angels. A week later, she began to see and hear them. She told me that the angels wanted me to write what they were saying. This is what we were told:

> *Tolerance. Have tolerance to understand what we are doing and why we are doing it; it is to teach the truth. The first step in learning the truth is opening up. This means opening up your consciousness to whatever plane you feel comfortable. Plane means level of understanding. Everyone's plane is different, and accordingly, everyone has a different lesson to learn. Her lesson is to be patient and understanding. Your lesson is to have sympathy for yourself, to be good to yourself, to trust and*

> *believe in yourself and to love yourself. Take these steps and you will be whole. Just be you.*
>
> *The Book and the pen both need to be cleansed. You are both chosen for this task. You are to be in a balanced state of consciousness, which is achieved by healing the emotional issues to free your Self. You are old souls and have been together in many lifetimes. This is destined to be.*

I began to doubt. The angel sensed it immediately, and I was told:

> *You are chosen and stop doubting. You have to learn to seek for information. This was your incomplete task in your past life. You kept a journal of your experiences and then in the end you began to doubt yourself and the truth. When you doubted, the blackness began to move in, you became frightened and left the work incomplete.*

The Lessons Begin

While I decided to take up the task of writing this book on the angels' behalf, I often found myself plagued with self-doubt and insecurity. At one point when I could not understand the application of the teachings on anger, I felt like giving up. I asked the Angel to give me a break for a while but was told "*The time is now or never.*" I then realized it was useless to ask for more time, and that I would have to stick to the basic teachings and wait for answers or clarification to come. They always did, and the lessons began.

Praying with Humility

We saw the Golden Angel kneeling with his hands folded in prayer. We asked the meaning of this and the angel replied, "We are constantly offering prayers of gratitude to the Creator." Prayers for the salvation, redemption and freedom of the human soul are constantly being offered up to the Creator. Angels are created to teach, serve and heal the human souls. We serve our Self first by understanding our life experiences to know the Self in turn life serves God itself.

Angels constantly pray to the Creator for the salvation and freedom of human souls; therefore, humans should constantly pray to the angels for the salvation and freedom of their own souls. We should always be grateful to the angels for what they provide. When a human prays with a humble heart, angels always hear and respond to these prayers. Angels always give us the answers we seek, but we do not always recognize them.

Past Lives

An individual's past-life may have unresolved emotions, beliefs, habits, karmic actions or painful death experiences. These experiences remain in the soul's memory (blueprints), and these same feelings, accompanied by emotions, are carried over into the present lifetime and require resolution. Life lessons, then, are an ongoing, continuous process. We are continually taught, from lifetime to lifetime until we achieve balance and wholeness and become one with the angels and God.

One of my past lives was revealed to me. In this past life, I was a young, innocent boy about sixteen years of age who worked as a slave – a scribe who wrote on stone tablets. My friend during this lifetime was a pharaoh in Egypt. The pharaoh, being greedy, cruel and egotistical, allowed himself to be ruled by his ego. His desire was to be popular. When I came too close to writing the truth about him, I was killed (beheaded). Because of my friend's role in this, being the pharaoh, her soul had to pay in subsequent lifetimes. Forms of redemption showed her to be very poor in other lifetimes, and once she was thrown into a pit and killed by dogs. She recognized her fear of dogs had carried over to this lifetime. The task became clear to us: we had to finish what we had begun. In other words, my friend and I had to make amends for our karmic burdens or debts in order to be debt-free towards each other.

I was told that I was too innocent to recognize darkness in people and that I thought everyone thought and believed as I did. I thought everyone had the same knowledge. My innocence did not permit me to see the difference between darkness and light, and I often told the truth to the wrong people. I was uncertain as to what was meant by innocence so I asked for an explanation. The angel replied, "*The innocent mind is when its negative conditioning no longer stimulates the brain; the mind becomes free and clear.*"

The angel continued to speak on this book and our involvement:

> *The task is incomplete, and it is her [her being my lady friend – she was the one who this time saw*

> *and heard the angels] payment to you by being a seer and a voice for the angels. Your task is to write and seek information. Seeking knowledge to know the truth is your purpose. Ask for healing through prayers when needed. You both have to finish this task. Trust each other; learn from the past and let it go. The important part of letting go is to forgive and to release. Now it is time to heal the past.*

We requested healing, one at a time. I especially asked healing for my ignorance of not being able to see the difference between black and white or darkness and light within human minds. I felt that I was still carrying this issue in my present lifetime. We prayed and thanked the angels for the healing. I also recognized the reason for always wanting to know the truth but never being able to find it. I have always had questions and have always searched for answers. With the help of the angels, I finally realized the truth was to be found within. All answers are found within oneself; absolutely no truth is found outside of us. The only thing outside of us is *Maya*, in which we are tempted to live because of our emotions and stains.

Maya is a word used in Hindu scripture to describe human attachment to material possessions, people, money and glory. Another meaning of *Maya* is "illusions of the physical world" from the soul's perspective. The material world is an illusion or a drama played out by our emotional issues. The truth lies under the veil of *Maya*.

Karma is cause and effect, positive and negative action taken by using our free will, or simply put, "what goes around, comes around". Accumulated, earned negative deeds from past-lives and the present life bring about a negative payback karmic time in our present life. Such an issue could be something as simple as anger. Anger harms the individual who is angry, not the person who is the object of the anger. Accumulated earned positive deeds from the past and present life, on the other hand, bring *sanskar* – a Sanskrit word used in Hindu scripture. This could be as simple as living life with a non-judgmental attitude.

We carry unlearned lessons, issues, *sanskar* and karma from past lives into the present lifetime to learn about them and work them out. An issue that has no bearing in this lifetime has to have belonged to some other lifetime. Because of this, whatever happens to us in our childhood is the effect of our *sanskar* or karma. Everything in our life is part of our earned journey, thus acceptance of our childhood experiences is the first step in the spiritual journey.

When I asked why some people see angels and others do not and wondered if the reason for this may be that we earn to have vision from a past-life's *sanskar*. I was told: "*It is not through the past life's privilege that you earn 'the right' to see angels. It is to be in the angel's timings that a person will have a vision; it has nothing to do with the timings on the physical plane.*"

We both decided that we did not want to carry the burden of our incomplete work into subsequent lives. It was either deal with our karmic debt now or face it in another lifetime. We chose to accept our responsibilities now rather than feel guilty for the rest of our lives. We were tasked with writing this book. My friend agreed to pass on the information the angels wanted me to write in their book, and I agree to write about these angelic teachings and instruction.

The Royal Battle

> *Please bubble the written material in this section, binding it in cords of Divine Light. None shall escape. All are rendered powerless by the all-knowing, all-seeing Creator. Cast all negativity into infinate love and light, never to return. Fill all spaces with Divine Sacred Light. We request cleansing and then its release into the care of the Divine Light of the Creator. Thank you.*

As everything in life should begin with prayer and gratitude, we prayed and asked the angels to tell us what lessons we needed to learn. We always lit a candle for protection and to show respect to the angels. The angels began by teaching us about our battles with negative entities. The Angel with a Hat – the hat represents the honour and responsibility that the angel carries for all souls' initial battle – and his troops took care of the initial battle and showed us how to destroy the negative entities. Responsibility was then returned to us, and he disappeared. The battle intensified, and we were given tools of Divine Intervention to help us defeat the negative entities. The angels kept watch and told us that *in the end the truth would win.*

The battle, itself, was somewhat similar to what I had recently seen in a movie where humans were fighting negative energies by engaging in physical combat. Mortals are no match for fighting negative energies in this manner. In reality, a human's physical strength is no match for negative entities; only the pure energy of the angels can be used to defeat and destroy the dark energy. Prayers are used as weapons. In our case, this was achieved by invoking the angels of different tasks and asking for various Divine Interventions until we were able to destroy the negative energy.

The dark energy was presented in many forms: a huge snake with seven heads (representing the seven stains of human ignorance), an enormous tree with long, large roots that held millions of souls captive, souls imprisoned in a dungeon, a giant beetle, a white angel in disguise, a black unicorn and others. Each time a dark entity was destroyed, millions of souls were freed and sent towards the Divine Light. When we felt stuck or asked for help, the angels were there giving subtle hints and providing Divine Intervention for stubborn entities. The giant beetle was the most difficult and took the longest time to destroy. When our prayers seemed not to work, we turned to the angels for help. The angel told us to be creative, but because of fear we found ourselves unable to think creatively. We thought of the Creator and took refuge beside God's throne for protection. Finally, the angel told us to ask Him to turn the beetle upside down, and then perform the prayer to bind, destroy, and cleanse. We did as instructed, and the beetle burst into a big ball of fire and disappeared. We thanked the angels for their assistance.

After the experiences, the negative attacks resulted in physical pain and headaches. Prayers for healing, protection and cleansing provided instant release. To say this was an unpleasant journey would be an understatement. It was very difficult, and we were anxious to see its end. Throughout the battle, we were tested for our intentions, the seven stains of ignorance, our understanding and appreciation of the protection prayer, and total trust and faith – both in ourselves and in the angels and God.

Every time a dark entity was destroyed, the angels and God would give us spiritual gifts – a small crown, a small pair of baby wings, a halo etc., – saying that we had earned them. We took the gifts, thanked the angels and God and then returned them for we knew it was truly the angels who had performed the tasks. This was a test of our ego. Please note that the angels, God and ascended souls, including Jesus, were watching us win this Royal Battle. The battle's name was given to us by an angel.

The battle was also a test of our ability to adhere to the truth. It taught us to recognize the disguises of dark entities and helped us to understand that the universe and the rest of the planes – including the physical plane – are in total balance with the two opposing energies. God, the angels and the rest of divine creation have their exact opposites (sometimes in disguise) in the universe. As above, so below – the two energies are not limited by time and space. They exist in the past, present and future simultaneously. The difference in experiencing the two energies is as follows:

1. God is the Creator of the soul and is connected with our soul. The negative energies create emotions and stains, rules our ego and is connected to the heart.
2. God gives us freedom of choice. The negative intimidates us with its power and control. It lures the soul away from God through the temptation of the seven stains of human

consciousness.

3. God's angels work through innocent human souls. The negative ruler's entities work through humans who have conceded to negative choices.
4. Experiences of God or the angels leave us in a peaceful, calm and balanced state. Experience with the negative energies creates imbalance and confusion.
5. Experience of Self occurs with a clear mind, clear thoughtforms and a profound understanding that sinks deep inside the soul and becomes a part of you. This realization makes perfect sense and creates harmony. Experiences of the heart involve emotions and stains that create confusion and cause unpleasant feelings. No understanding is gained, but lessons can be learned. The human ego is always involved.

6. God and the angels know all, so do the negative energy and its entities.

> *Please bubble the above-written material in this section, binding it in cords of Divine Light. None shall escape. All is rendered powerless by the all-knowing, all-seeing Creator who casts all negativity into infinate love and light, never to return, filling all spaces with Divine Sacred Light. We request its cleansing and its release into the care of Divine Light of the Creator. Thank you.*

This journey taught us to pray constantly. An angel asked what I intended to do with the information and the teachings they gave me. I remained quiet because I did not have an answer. The only thing I wanted to do was learn and know the truth about life. Then the angel asked, "*Is it to gain name, fame, success and wealth?*" I shook my head in disagreement because I could not even imagine writing a book about angels. At that time I lacked knowledge and understanding and had little confidence in myself. To think of name, fame and success was absurd!

The angels tested us by giving us this current book about their teachings, already in written form. We had to go through a journey to protect the book from the negative entities, after which we returned the book to the angels. We were tested many times for our stains, mainly ego. Because of this, we had to constantly think of our tests on all levels before we took anything from the angels. For example, we could have kept the book, but we gave it back because it was not ours and we did not deserve it. If we had allowed ourselves to be influenced by ego, we would have wrongly kept the book.

The Blue Angel said, "*Your search is over, and your journey has just begun.*" We continued to receive the basic structure of the angels' teachings over a period of about a year. The angels knew that I was not applying the teachings in my present life so they started to wean us off by saying, "*We have given you what you need; the rest will be provided when the lessons are being learned.*" I caused myself more disappointment by insisting that more information be given me. But it was time for me to *apply* the teachings. Although the angels were always firm and showed me my issues, I just could not seem to grasp them.

The Blue Angel reminded me:

> *You've got to get the grip of the truth. You are not practising what the angels have taught you. You don't stop to look, feel and see. You don't analyze everything in life, about life. Ask, seek and find the answers. You have two faces: you say and feel two different things. Feel deeper while you speak. Speak through your heart. Put your heart where your mouth is.*
>
> *You have no faith, no trust and you do not self-question. You do not have total commitment, devotion or respect and gratitude. Have faith. Faith means unquestioning, undoubting commitment and belief. Learn loyalty, trust and see the truth. Use them. Learn to have patience, tolerance and acceptance.*

I still found myself unable to do much with the teachings. I tried very hard, but seemed to veer in the wrong direction. At times when I felt like giving up, I would hear the Blue Angel's words: "*You give up too soon.*" The angels were giving me answers, but I failed to recognize them. The angels give us directions so that we may find the answers ourselves. We are not spoon-fed, and because of this, we must work hard on the Self to learn our lessons. Although I did not feel that I was learning, everything the angels were saying registered into my soul. I could feel that as the angels spoke, the words would penetrate my being and sink deeper within until they became a part of my Self.

Finally, the angels questioned each of us about our purpose in life and what we chose to do with their teachings. My friend chose to return to her former way of life and decided to have nothing further to do with the teachings. She gave back their teachings, and the angels took them by erasing them from her memory. I replied: "I am going to follow the teachings, learn my lessons and find out what my life's purpose is." In 1996, my friend and I parted to embark on separate, chosen journeys. Eventually we both left the city, and our lives moved in different directions.

I could sense great empathy in the angel's voice when I asked why my friend chose to walk away. The angel said, "*There are many choices and many lessons to be learned. She has the freedom to choose. You made the same choice in your childhood and you learned.*" I agreed and understood. Then in the same empathetic voice the Angel said, "*It is going to be a very lonely journey for you. You can choose what you want as long as you don't make tokens* (money) *your life's purpose; ego begets tokens.*"

The past two years have been a very lonely, difficult journey, but it has been a learning and earning one. Truth was presented as a lesson or experience, and I had to go through a process of physically enduring the lesson and then reaching a point of understanding where I could live in total and absolute acceptance. I then went through the process of emotional healing – freeing and healing the Self so that I might arrive at a balanced state of consciousness. Practice indeed makes perfect, and I often perfected my lessons by repetition.

I realized that the angels' patience and tolerance had taught me to view my issues as lessons. I recognized that I had gained understanding and acceptance on all four levels: physical (whatever was happening), emotional (how I was reacting to the situation), intellectual (recognizing the root of the issue) and spiritual (healing the issues). It then dawned on me that this is the purpose of every experience presented by an angel. Humbly, I prayed to the angels and asked that they not give up on me for I felt that I was a slow learner. I made certain that I gave thanks and showed gratitude, no matter how difficult the learning experience. During a time like this and in this state of mind, we are more open and receptive to learning, and the lessons flow freely.

This Book – The Angels' Book

The Blue Angel said, "*All your thought-forms belong to us. All emotions and stains are yours, and all thought-forms operated under the influence of stains and emotions are yours.*" I learned that all wisdom, knowledge and intelligence created by our thought-forms belong to the angels and God. As messengers of God, angels have been passing divine wisdom and teachings to human souls since the beginning of time. Throughout history many souls have been chosen for instruction, and many have reached a state of balance and wholeness vital to attaining the freedom and salvation of the soul. Human consciousness is rising constantly, and many souls are perceiving angelic teachings and are walking the path of balanced consciousness at this present time. Because all of the answers I receive in my thought-forms belong to the angels, I genuinely feel this book belongs to the angels – just as our soul belongs to the Creator.

I was informed by the Blue Angel: "*The biggest battle will be the book. The negative beings are not ready to receive, to hear, to accept, to listen and obey. Draw the sign of a cross or a sword on the book for your protection. Your job is to finish the book as a warrior, as a messenger for the angels. Once the battle is fought for one, it is fought for all souls. Once the teachings are imparted to one soul, they are imparted to all.*" Other angels, God and Jesus continued to counsel and encourage me. Jesus exhorted: "*Have faith! Don't give up; believe in the Creator, in yourself, in the Book, in freedom of choices and in the salvation of man (the soul). Believe that God shall win.*" The White Angel urged me to remember that "*When doubt creeps in, you lose your balance. Doubting means doubting in Self, doubting in God and in the angels. Trust, affirm, be sincere and believe. Become one with the angels.*"

I had no idea how to write a book so I asked for direction. The angel said, "*Yes, the book depends on your intention. We gave other humans the information, and they backed down, losing their spot. Nobody knows the truth to the extent that you know.*" I felt sad and worried because I did not think that I knew enough truth. The angel realized my thoughts and asked, "*Who is sad? You are sad, and you worry too much. You will be provided with everything that you are going to need.*"

The Creator[10] said,

> *What you seek and as you seek,* ***ask****. All will be revealed to you. You are too innocent; you must learn to tell the difference between positive and negative energies. Seek out pure thought-forms for everyone by imagining them in a blue light. The thought-forms are no longer your attachments but responsibilities. Respect the balance. Learn the frail attachments of human consciousness.*

10 Many times, the spiritual beings would identify themselves. Other times, if they did not, I would ask their identity either at the beginning or end of our conversations.

I recognize and embrace the truth of these words. In the past years, my understanding has grown and through my "lessons in learning", I have come to realize that the angels' teachings are a completion of the truth. Now I not only have the knowledge of the truth but also the realization of the truth through life's experiences.

All that I have asked has been revealed to me. For instance, when I asked, "What did you mean by 'losing the spot'?" – referring to information given earlier in this chapter – the angel replied, "*It simply means that if you choose to walk away from the task we have asked you to do, then we move on to prepare another soul to do it.*" I realized that earning salvation of the soul is not easy and losing it can be very easy. I simply had to respond "no" or choose to walk away.

In 1998, my heart and soul would not settle down to do anything else – my soul kept reminding me to start writing the book. But my physical situation, my day-to-day living, kept pointing me towards going to work. I felt I was being pulled in two directions, and I had to make a decision. Writing the book became my priority so I began this journey with the angels. Making the decision to follow God's will and my soul's desire led me to discover my freedom of Self, wholeness and complete oneness with God in a circle of Divine Light.

If you recognize any new awakening in yourself,
give thanks to the angels for their wisdom and
the knowledge they provide.

The Seven Stains of Human Ignorance

Please protect, bless and cleanse the following chapter. Thank you.

THE EXPRESSION OF THE HIGHER SELF is to recognize the seven stains of human ignorance. These stains are the negative traits of human consciousness, which are ego, anger, lust, attachment, greed, hatred and jealousy. Through these stains we cause pain, suffering, hurt, harm to ourselves or to other living souls. Usually this happens without our realizing that retribution will catch up to us sooner or later. In other words, we cannot hurt another without hurting ourselves. Sometimes the payback seems to be many times heavier than the actual act. During this difficult time of retribution if we recognize and accept where we have gone wrong, it becomes a "lesson in learning".

Each stain has seven levels, which require work. Each level is further divided into seven sub-levels. The last levels of the stains are illusory and deceiving. They are difficult to detect without the angels' help and wisdom. All humans have the seven stains in varying degrees. The human ego needs these stains in order to survive. One has to be extremely prudent about the stains and keep requesting the angels, in our prayers, for awareness of the stains. These stains are also called *human temptations* and *human frailties*.

Human ignorance is the reason we fail to recognize the stains we possess. The Blue Angel said, "*Freedom of Self comes from recognizing and healing the stains and their underlying emotions.*" We must recognize and start working on these stains and begin healing the feelings prior to the emotion taking over our mind; this can be a long process. The soul will be tested many times by the angels until even the slightest temptation has been removed from our consciousness.

Some of the stains have deep, underlying, inner feelings arising from our soul's issues. We need to analyze these feelings in order to feel and heal our soul. If we are not accustomed to examining our underlying feelings, we quickly pass them to our ego or stains. For example, if we feel helpless in a certain situation, we may begin to think that it is someone else's fault. We become angry and blame others. Our ego prevents us from seeing that the fault or issue is our own. This becomes a negative, outer projection of inner feelings. This attitude leads us to transform feeling of helplessness into one of anger.

We may feel that we are protecting ourself, but we will progress more rapidly in the healing of our stains if we work on our inner feelings. We must look inward for answers because everything in life begins with the Self – the soul, spirit, True Self, or Higher Self. By looking inward, we assume responsibility for our True Self, and this prevents us from reacting with judgment and blame (anger). We should keep in mind that all stains are interconnected with our ego or our false or illusory Self. As the Blue Angel explained: "*Once you are stained with one, you are stained with all seven.*"

Here are some examples of the underlying feelings of some of the stains. Ego, the illusory self, has a fundamental inner feeling of lack of self, which includes knowledge of self, self-respect, self-esteem, self-worth and so on. Lack of Self promotes feelings of emptiness, insecurity, defensiveness and non-existence – the conviction that life has no meaning. If we look inwardly, we are prompted to know the true Self. If we look outwardly to fill this need, our illusory self takes over and we move in a negative direction to fulfill these desires from the physical world.

Anger has causal, inner feelings of helplessness and hurt. This is the soul's birth issue: we are born helpless with sole reliance, on our mother for nurturing. If we overlook these feelings, we may become angry and judgmental. We often blame others for our situation. Attachment has a core issue of loneliness. Our soul feels lonely, alone and sad without the love and light of God. The love is ever present but hidden under the veil of our ego or *Maya*. Our soul is not always able to communicate with our heart and mind because our ego prevents it. In such instances, we are unable to hear the gentle whispers of the soul.

Lust has an underlying issue of lack of self-love. Greed, hatred and jealousy are basically the negative aspects of our anger and illusory self.

The angel advised: "*Stains are part of the personality and emotions of the human consciousness in the physical world. Ig-*

norance means: failing to comprehend, distinguish and recognize these stains." Stains blend well into our daily habits, behaviour and emotional issues, which is why they are difficult to recognize and change. We must commit ourselves to this search for truth.

Ego

The Golden Angel said: "*Ego puts you on a mountain, and then it knocks you down the mountain. People put you on a pedestal; if you accept it, the fall is sure to come. Ego is the balance* (opposite) *of humility and acceptance. The balance of ignorance is awareness.*"

The human ego is the hardest stain with which to work. It is the primary stain that works with a combination of the rest of the stains. Our egos feel wounded when we are shown our lacks, weaknesses, habits, stains, etc. It hurts because the ego's origin is in the heart. Wounded ego often reacts by projecting its own issues, needs and demands onto others. When ego and anger dominate the personality, an individual has difficulty accepting or recognizing these stains in him or herself.

As the Blue Angel explains: "*Ego has an automatic defence mechanism to protect through the stains. This gives birth to stubbornness and blame in that a human puts their own negative thought-forms onto others.*"

Denial is always an act of our ego. Instead of accepting our mistakes, habits, patterns and wrongdoings, we may blame and find fault in others. It is always easier to place blame than to face our issues or problems. What we do not realize is that these issues or experiences will repeat again and again until the lesson has been learned. Sometimes the problem is simply ignorance of the fact that ego stands in our way and does not allow us to admit our shortcomings.

Ego, with its stains, patterns and emotional issues, is connected to the physical or material world. We often call this '*baggage*'. The angel called it "garbage", and I was told that these stains were mine alone. The angel did promise to heal me when I was ready to accept responsibility and move on to learning and healing my issues.

The Blue Angel said, "*Denial is manipulation of the emotions and excuses. If you are about to make an excuse, you should know that excuses are not valid. It is only to save the face of the ego at the expense of betraying your Self.*"

The Functions of Soul,[11] Heart and Mind

Soul

The Self is free: free from all negative conditioning. It has unconditional love, divine communication and pure and clear thought-forms. Our soul knows, feels and sees everything inside and outside of us. Our soul, being a part of God, is pure, positive and immortal. But on earth, the soul is imprisoned in a human body. It is not free to communicate through our heart and mind when the illusory self overwhelms us with its emotional issues and stains. This is one reason we feel sadness and hurt deep within our souls. Our souls long to be free and be with its Creator. Gut feelings stem from the soul. They may be feelings of sadness, pain, loneliness – sometimes like a stab-

11 The Self is the term used for the soul, spirit, True Self and Higher Self.

bing wound or a deep desire for truth, freedom, peace, serenity, gratitude, humility and love. The soul's unconditional love for God will never betray us. Once we experience this love, we cannot help but share it. Every soul on earth is on its journey towards wholeness, whether we are aware of it or not.

The Golden Angel said, "*Knowing and freeing the Self brings about love for the Self; self-trust, self-belief, faith and loyalty to the angels' teachings and to the Self.*"

Heart

The angel made sure that I understood the difference between heart, soul and mind. I was told that all my emotional issues and stains (ego, anger, attachment, lust, greed, hatred, and jealousy) belonged to my heart. The heart's emotional issues cause a lot of suffering on the physical plane. Love and trust originating from the heart's needs and desires (attachment) can be betrayed. We must allow our Higher Self to take charge of our heart by working through and healing these issues and stains. By doing so, our minds are more able to distinguish clearly between negative and positive thought-forms. From this vantage point, we can influence our decisions from our soul's desire. When we reach this stage, our mind, heart and soul become aligned with God's Divine Light. We become one with the angels and God and reach a balanced state of consciousness. Our heart becomes a sacred heart immersed with Divine Love and Light because our soul operates through our heart without the interception of ego. The angels referred to it as a circle of God's Divine Light with all three: the angels, God and us within it or our heart, mind and soul in a circle of Divine Love and Light.

When the physical body dies, our emotional issues and stains die. This can be explained in an out-of-body experience where the soul is free and unlimited. We view things from the soul's perspective. After this experience the soul has a greater understanding of what we need to learn and change. This experience totally changes our views about life because the soul awakens while living in the physical body. This experience teaches us to distinguish between the desires of the soul and the heart.

I was told that there are two mirrors facing each other: one in our heart and one in our soul. The soul's feeling (image) is picked up by the mirror in the heart, for example, feelings of hurt and helplessness, but the illusory self, which operates through the heart while in the physical world, will force us to look for answers outside. We react to the situation, and it becomes an inner struggle between negative and positive choices. Confusion arises when we are unable to distinguish between the soul's feelings and reactions from the heart. These stains and emotional issues, however, play a very important role in our lives. We experience them, enjoy them (as our attachments), learn from them and then heal them when circumstances change in our lives.

Mind or Intellect

The mind is the decision maker. It processes our negative and positive thoughts, which it receives from our Higher Self and our illusory self. We have free will and as such, are free to choose between the heart and soul's needs, wants, desires and wishes. We tend to make decisions based on emotion. We work on the Self by practising refusal to submit to negative choices (emotions).

The White Angel instructed: "*The conscious mind is a human factor when emotions overwhelm the individual; the mind gets clouded and an individual becomes confused. The unconscious mind is connected to the Self, which gives us a clear understanding and positive choices. Keep your head above the emotions; don't let them drag you down.*"

To this day, my struggle with my illusory self occurs when I have made a decision from my soul's desire. My illusory self takes over and presents me with an idea as to what to do next. I often have mental conversations where I say that I don't care to do this or that, or I simply say "no, thank you," and the idea disappears. Not all ideas are negative, but if the goal behind the idea is centered only on material gain (greed) and refusal to see its potential for causing harm to others, then it is decidedly negative. I find that by taking a deep breath instantly shuts off the connection of illusory self and connects me to my higher self and the very first thought remains intact.

The Difference between Higher Self and Illusory Self

We know truth and know who we really are from the soul. Our soul has positive energy that makes us respond in a positive manner. The feelings of the soul are much deeper than the heart. We are encouraged to think deeply and search within for answers. When our hearts are overwhelmed with emotional issues and stains, it weighs heavily on our chest and we feel the need to find release by talking or having someone listen. These feelings from our illusory self are on the surface and we want to project them outwardly, which is a negative reaction.

I began to reflect on how, why and when I started to give in to my illusory self, and I asked the angel about this. I was shown an early childhood experience, around the age of four, of being lost in a jungle. I describe this experience in greater detail in Chapter 6. From the experience, I was able to understand that the soul is born in the physical body with all of the "Power of Self": self-love (the unconditional love of God), self-belief, self-trust, self-respect, self-worth, faith, loyalty, truth, honesty and integrity. As we grow older we give the "Power of Self" to our negative choices (ego, the false self that resides in our heart) although we never lose the "Power of Self." For me, this occurred because of a traumatic childhood experience where I was left feeling totally helpless, confused, fearful, alone, hungry, thirsty and exhausted from crying and walking. I created this situation because of my adventurous spirit. When confusion clouded my mind, fear set in. I gave up and gave way to negative choices. This set a pattern and created an emotional issue, which repeated for the rest of my life until I got to know myself and healed the issues of my heart and soul through prayers to the angels.

We can be forever lost in the game that our ego plays with us. Without the angels' healing of our emotional issues and stains, it is not possible to come out of this cycle. In Hindu philosophy, the play of ego, the rest of the stains and our emotional issues are known as the "play of *Maya*". Every individual is on his or her own journey but not necessarily a journey of finding the truth. *Maya* relates to the material world. *Maya* is the ego's material comforts, for example, fame, gain, loss, love, family, friends, happiness etc. Our ego creates the illusory *Maya*. In *Maya* everything is temporary and subject to change over time. From the soul's point of view, absolutely nothing is real in *Maya*. Rather it is a tool used to show us the difference between our choices so that eventually we can learn to know our real Self. We have come alone, and we will go alone; we arrived with our soul only, and we will depart as a soul. Absolutely nothing that we create and become attached to on this earth goes with us.

During the course of life's experiences, we may often feel a sense of emptiness or loneliness. We may feel unloved, sad and unfulfilled. These are the feelings of lack of self that are painful and cause us to suffer greatly. We feel distanced from God's love and light; it is still present, but not available until we earn it back. This is God's and the angels' way of telling us to return to the original choice and bring back the "Power of Self." When we renew this decision, the spiritual journey begins. No matter what choices we make, there are no right or wrong choices; they are all "lessons in learning".

Soul – The Higher Self

The Soul is our awareness; it is the pure love and light of the Creator within. The soul has clarity and pure thought-forms. Through the soul's inner senses we experience God and the angels by knowing, seeing, understanding, hearing, touching (feeling), tasting and smelling. Although it is very hard to tell the difference between the outer and inner senses, the memory of the inner experience is imprinted on our soul and remains eternally.

Our soul can attain acceptance, humility, serenity, gratitude, honesty, truth, respect, loyalty, detachment, peace and balance. The soul can attain power of Self that includes self-determination, belief, trust, faith, respect, discipline, worth, loyalty, and self-love – ultimately, the unconditional love of God.

Our soul can be set free from the bondage of the physical world, illusory self, emotional issues, stains, pain, hurt, sadness and suffering. We can become free from all negativity while living in the physical body. The purpose of the spiritual journey is to know the Self by healing the emotional issues and stains generated from our heart. By healing the Self, we regain the "Power of Self," which was once given over to negative choices.

Ego The Illusory Self

Ego is the human consciousness that belongs to the physical body and physical world. It operates through our outer senses such as taste, touch, smell, sight and hearing. Ego is me, myself, and I. It is self-centered, selfish and self-gratifying. Our ego will prompt us to seek physical and material gain.

Ego betrays the Self. We feel a lack of Self and, not knowing how to fill this lack, we try to feed on outside, material sources. Our ego often interferes with the Soul, and we need to recognize this fact. When ego operates through us we have little respect for ourselves and others; we have none of the Self. The result is insecurity, frustration and disappointment. We often feel empty inside, and to make ourselves feel special, we may try to prove we are better than others in order to satisfy our ego.

Ego works with the combination of the rest of the stains in

varying degrees. This individualizes each soul. Ego has a huge appetite, and it satisfies its hunger through anger, attachment, lust, greed, hatred and jealousy. The resulting emotional trauma works its way through our heart as pain, anguish, shame, guilt, confusion, fear and despair. When these feelings arise, our childhood emotional issues surface and require resolution. By dealing with these issues, we set the soul free and experience the healed, real Self. We release ourselves from hurt, pain and suffering through a "lesson in learning". Lessons in learning can also be referred to as experiencing the issue with an understanding from the soul's viewpoint.

When our ego gets hurt, our hidden hurts surface, and we sometimes project our insecurities onto others in the form of anger, blame and judgment. We defend our ego in this manner in order to keep it intact. Ego is always in competition with others.

The following is a comparison between ego, the false self and the soul, the Higher Self.

Ego (the False Self) versus the Soul (the Higher Self)

- Ego is negative, toxic, false, and superficial. Soul is positive, pure, and our true self.
- Ego is supposedly confident. Soul has self-determination.
- Ego is illusory, destructive, deceptive and manipulative and obtains control through fear. Soul is clear, simple, honest and filled with integrity and love.
- Ego is always judging, blaming and finding fault. Soul makes no judgments.
- Ego has many desires and makes choices through its stains.

Soul has one desire and one choice: to know God.
- Ego is in a constant battle with our soul. We must recognize this and choose accordingly.

Ego's Hatred and Jealousy

Hatred and jealousy are two states of human ignorance whose worst trait is anger. They are created by overpowering negativity and submission to negative choices. The mind becomes conditioned by negative thought-forms. An angry individual always thinks that the other person is the cause of this anger. This is true to the extent that this individual or an incident triggers a suppressed, painful, emotional childhood issue. The aggressive, resentful, angry mind is so full of negativity, impatience and destruction that it rejects listening, feeling and understanding. This gives birth to hatred and jealousy. The individual reacts with cruelty, revenge, suspicion, judgment, disrespect, unkindness and even violent behaviour without conscience – simply for disliking a person or situation in order to satisfy the hunger of his or her ego. When the anger subsides, the individual may decide there are alternatives or other choices. If the anger remains, then this becomes the individual's lesson and consequences become a result of action.

Ego's Greed

As we examine the interconnections of all seven stains, we recognize that ego generates the remainder of the stains for survival and dominance. Greed is the uncontrolled and immoderate desire for wealth and pleasure. It is connected to the ego as name, fame and social status. Avaricious people cling to wealth and material possessions (attachment). If greed is present, it will perpetuate the action of multiplying wealth. Actions out of greed are created without conscience and result in selfishness, self-centeredness, unscrupulousness, dishonesty and discontent.

The balance of greed is contentment, honesty and integrity. While there is nothing wrong with living comfortably with contentment, honesty and simplicity, greed breeds excess and unhealthy attachment to the material rather than spiritual.

Ego's Lust

Lust is an emotional, impulsive urge for sexual fulfillment. It takes the form of a desperate need for love, which seeks emotional satisfaction. It can be overpowering and difficult to master once the mind comes under its control and hormonal influence. This form of desire is generated by the ego because of a lack of "self love". Deep within our souls, we feel we are lacking the unconditional love of God. Since the ego is connected only to the shallow levels of the heart and the outer senses of the physical world, it prevents us from looking deeper within the Self. We look to others for gratification. Such is the, "temptation of lust".

The balance of lust is self-love. Once we start to feel love for Self, through the healing of our heart and soul issues, the intense desire of lust lessens or even disappears; only true love remains.

Ego's Attachment

Attachment is the opposite polarity of the Power of Self: self-trust, self-respect, self-love, self-acceptance, self-reliance, self-belief, self-determination and self-worth. While attachments may be extensive in number, simply put, anything in the physical world that emotionally upsets us adds to our attachments or issues. Examples include emotional issues, stains, patterns, habits, material possessions, beliefs (religious, cultural and social), people (family, friends, social circle, relationship, idols, etc.), pets, surroundings, career, wealth, fame and so on. Any emotion or anything that we cannot release is an attachment.

The White Angel elaborated: "*All friendships and other relations are attachments. They are only labels. You cannot be a true friend to anyone unless you are true to yourself. By labelling anything and anyone, you claim them and they become your attachments. Attachments are false identities.*"

The Golden Angel continued: "*True friendship is unconditional, unbiased, honest, totally accepting, and non judgmental. It is a mutual trust, not being taken advantage of and loyal.* [A friend is] *the one who can make us see the truth in life rather than supporting the negative habits and emotions. Friendship lasts on equality, maturity, fairness and care for each other. Friendship loses its ground when human factors start to get involved* (stains); *at the same time, spirituality loses its ground and* [the relationship] *ends in judgments.*"

The Blue Angel advised: "*Learn about your frail attachments of human consciousness. Everything in life has to be unconditional without judgment; if not, it is an attachment.*"

Attachment on its last level comes in the form of love. There is a fine line between emotional human love and God's unconditional love. Human love provides a temporary happiness, which never completely satisfies and always creates desire for more. When loved ones leave or die, it causes enormous hurt, pain and suffering. Unconditional love is eternal joy and peace. Our soul is unaffected by emotions; it always lives in acceptance, learning and understanding.

Personal Lessons Related to Ego

My instruction began with learning about my ego, anger and judgment. I was shown a picture of a little girl with her hands covering her eyes. The Blue Angel said, "*The little girl is in great denial. She is not seeing because she doesn't want to see. She has no trust, faith, sincerity, loyalty or gratitude. She wanted to get the credit* [for her experience explained below] *and was looking for status and honour, yet she didn't want to acknowledge and accept* [that this would just feed her ego]. *The little girl has always been in denial; her ego is betraying her soul.*"

I felt as if I had been hit by bolt of lightning; the pain was tremendous. I was shocked and uncomprehending because I did not think that I had a big problem with my ego. But deep within, I sensed the truth of the angel's words. For the next two weeks I worked hard on this issue, but it took five years before I was able to resolve and release all seven levels of these stains. To this day, I know that I will be tested repeatedly for these stains until my physical body leaves its existence.

Intuitively, I recognized the description of the little girl; it represented my childhood experience with God, and the angel was describing its after-effects. I decided now is the time for understanding and analysis. Now is the time to ask questions and seek angelic wisdom. I asked for forgiveness of my ignorance, and asked for complete comprehension of the experience and healing for the little girl's heart. This experience occurred about forty-three years ago, yet it has remained as fresh in my memory as if it happened yesterday.

I was about ten or twelve years of age at the time. I remember my father telling me, "If you want to know something, you must concentrate on it." Being raised in a Hindu family and seeing my mother praying to all these gods and goddesses, I was very curious to know which *one* of so many was the real God. After all, I need only to concentrate on one as my father told me to do. It was a bright afternoon when I sat down in my mother's prayer room. With this question in my mind, I closed my eyes. Soon I started to see in my mind's eye (soul), dark clouds moving out of my forehead and the space becoming clearer and clearer until it became pure white. This pure, white light consisted of millions of stars that came in through the top of my head and bathed me down to my feet. I felt pure, peaceful and filled with absolute joy and love. I did not want to leave this experience. I now understand these lights were angels cleansing and purifying my heart, mind, body, thought-forms and spirit (soul).

I spent some time bathing in the light's peace and unconditional love. Then I felt a kind of suction on the top of my head that brought me in front of a pure and extremely bright shaft of white light. It took a little while for my eyes to adjust to the light's brilliance. Suddenly, the shaft of light spoke: "*I am God. Ask what you want to know.*" At this point I was confused because I expected God to have a face and body (from my handed-down religious beliefs). Confused, I did not know what to ask. Then God said, "*Whatever you want, your wishes will be fulfilled.*"

I began to think. The only thing that came to mind was my initial thought concerning the real God. I said, "I want to know who the real God is." (This is the reason I have now come to know God within by knowing my Self.) God gave me more time to think of any other requests. There were a few material wishes going through my head, but I did not ask for them. My soul did not allow my ego to interfere. I understood that God had granted my wish. I stayed in God's light for a while, then the experience ended, and I opened my eyes.

The high-energy field of God's bliss stayed with me for several days. I felt weightless, as if I was floating. I was extremely excited about my experience. From sheer excitement and ignorance of ego, I hurried to tell my sisters about my experience. Instead of believing me, they mockingly told me that I must have been dreaming, lying, or trying to prove myself better than them. Then one of my sisters, speaking from religious beliefs, asked, "Why would God want to come to you? It only comes to the highly realized souls such as masters or saints." In my sister's view, I was unworthy to have an encounter with God, and I had no answer for her question.

I was hurt by this incident. I remember crying for a couple of days and asking God "Why?" Obviously my ego was hurting, but I did not realize this at that time. Much later, I came to realize that the experience was given me so that I might know my Self, believe in Self, trust in Self and be grateful to God. I realized it mattered not whether anyone else believed me, but that I alone believed. My ego, however, had caused me to fall flat on my face!

My hurting ego caused me to create a defence mechanism to protect the stains. This further gave birth to anger, stubbornness and blaming. In turn, I gave my negative thought-forms to God by being angry and saying, "Why did you give me this experience when no one believes in you? I do not want this experience because I do not understand the meaning of your giving it to me in the first place." Out of ignorance and fear, I chose to walk away. I was simply unprepared to listen and follow that particular path. I seemed to have forgotten or to have not fully realized that *I, myself,* had asked for this experience to know God. The experience, however, remained in my heart, mind and soul.

I always searched for answers and tried to understand the meaning of this childhood experience. Little did I know that some day the angels would provide answers. This would be when my lessons were learned and earned as I became more seriously committed to knowing myself and knowing truth. It has been a difficult lesson for my ego, and it took a long time to earn back the angels' teachings. We earn things back in the angels' time and when we are ready.

While I walked away from angelic teachings, the angels' never left me. I would continue to experience them often throughout my childhood. The angel had taught me about choices, I listened but did not follow them. It seems I was given many chances to get back on the path to truth, but I was unable to because of lack of Self, fear, disbelief and a lack of faith. Out of fear of being different, I made the negative choice of giving away the Power of Self.

Lack of Self proved to be major issue for me throughout my life. The patterns were repeated with different situations and people, but the lessons remained the same. Every lesson caused more hurt, pain and suffering. Through these experiences I came to realize that self-trust, faith and belief would be required to gain back the Power of Self.

During my childhood I thought that the Blue Angel was God because of how the energy felt. I recognized the Blue Angel because of his voice and the manner in which he taught. As I mentioned in Chapter Three, his voice and manner of teaching were the same. He appeared to me in human form and was dressed in the traditional, white clothing of Indian males so I felt quite comfortable in his presence. As I became more accustomed to the presence of angels, it no longer mattered to me whether I saw them or not. I now hear angels in my thoughtforms more often than seeing them.

It is important to note that the angels and God view us as a soul. There is no difference whether the soul is that of a child or an adult. In our soul, we know and understand certain things regardless of age. A soul's age is determined by its Book of Life, which is written by the White Angel.

As a child, I tried to excuse myself from learning, by saying that I was incapable of understanding angelic teachings. The Blue Angel answered, "*If you weren't capable of understanding then, it will be the same in the present time. Your own hands created all your sufferings, as you made your choice.*" I knew this to be true because I was indeed capable of understanding the teachings as a child, just as I did now as an adult. At the time, I simply made excuses because I was unwilling to learn. I chose to walk away, and as an adult, I found myself in the same situation, with the same feelings. I asked the angels to give me more time to understand their teachings, but I was succinctly told by the Blue Angel, "*You are trying to walk away again; you give up too soon. The time is now or never. The time will not return in this lifetime or in the next several lifetimes."*

I realized that this was my last opportunity to deal with my issues and that introspection, patience and persistence would be necessary. I knew the answers would come if I looked within. The Blue Angel suggested that I work out my issues by writing and promised: "*We will come through the writings to give you guidance, answers and healing" Your ego must be constantly balanced on both the conscious and unconscious, physical and spiritual levels.*" This meant that I would be tested for temptation on both levels.

The Blue Angel is very serious about teaching – always direct and never repeats what has been said. If I do not follow the teaching, the payback is instantaneous and powerful. For example if I was having negative thought-forms about someone while cooking, I got burned or cut my finger. I became a fast learner.

I was told: "*When you are learning, you cannot be earning.*" Although I worked and studied, my spiritual learning was prolonged because I often shifted my focus from Self to the world. I believe that if it had not been for the Blue Angel's strictness and patience, I would never have taken the teachings seriously or learned anything. I learned discipline, respect, patience, persistence, tolerance and, most of all, I learned to listen attentively so that I could follow the inner teachings.

While being taught to recognize ego, I was told: "*You have two faces; feel deeper while you speak. Speak through your heart. Put your heart where your mouth is.*" I was having difficulty acknowledging underlying feelings of hurt and helplessness and connecting them to emotional issues. We tend to suppress memories, especially if they are unpleasant. When we speak without taking the time to feel our hurt and pain, we are not speaking our truth. It is simply paying lip service for the sake of our ego or from learned behaviour. I discovered I was not looking in the right place for my answers.

My analysis of my ego differed from that of the angels, but I knew the angels were knowledgeable and recognized things I was unable to see myself. In my ignorance, I told the Angel that I did not completely (one hundred percent) believe in my experience. The Blue Angel gave this response: "*You were telling your sisters so they would acknowledge you and value you (ego), not because you did not believe one hundred percent what you have experienced.*" I realized this to be true for had I not believed, why would I continue to search for answers throughout my life? I responded that I was looking for confirmation because I truly felt that my sisters might have had similar experiences. The Angel said, "*You only seek confirmation when you have a lack of belief, trust and faith in Self. Follow your instincts; trust what you are being told. All confirmation comes from within, not from without. Take total charge of Self. Make a promise and peace with your Self in order to gain the freedom of Self.*"

The Blue Angel continued his instruction: "*Ego on its last level is extremely illusory. Beware of the titles that people put on one another. You accept the titles because of human frailties. Beware of false personalities, prophets, masters, teachers, healers, guides, words [writing] and demonstrations; any one of them can be an example of ego. Half knowledge is ego.*"

We must always remember that everything we have in life is a blessing from God. Any and everything we accomplish is through the help of God. Angels fulfill our choices, whether from the material or spiritual world. We must not claim credit for things that are of and from God. In the above paragraph, I was warned not to claim title or credit for my work on earth. The Angel warned me again and said, "*Be careful of the book "Emotional Healing with the Angels" becoming your ego. You can choose what you want as long as tokens are not your life's purpose. One of the last levels of the stains is temptation. A slightest temptation will lead you to deception and confusion. Your needs will always be provided for. It is the temptation that you need to overcome.*"

The truth is often painful because it unmasks the ego and reveals our stains in order to penetrate the Higher Self. The ego feels threatened, hurt, angry and reactive because it thinks it is the only Self we have. It feels threatened and endangered. I reacted in precisely this manner when the angels first began to teach me about my stains. The Blue Angel advised "*Lessons start early in life; it is up to you to mould your conscience.*" My next lessons would be on anger, its causes and how best to deal with it.

While recently praying, I asked God what was the best way to avoid the slightest temptation of the ego. The answer came: always create positive thought-forms. If negative thoughts or fear walk in, give yourself time by taking a deep breath. Then change your thought-form to a positive outcome by using your imagination or positive affirmations. Always analyze situations before responding or taking a course of action. Then let go or release it to God. Remove yourself from listening, seeing (judging) and participating in any negative conversation.

How to Work with Anger

The human ego can cause an individual to live in a state of non-acceptance or denial where excuses are readily made for shortcomings. Anger often results, and blame is unfairly and wrongly placed by projecting our own faults, issues or negative thought-forms on others. We become critical, judgmental and fault-finding. Ego causes us to be angry, argumentative, controlling, arrogant, condescending, intimidating, ignorant, impatient, anxious and excitable.

The Blue Angel cautioned: "*Blaming others is a projection of your own irresponsibility of your Self. To be angry with others is a projection of your own anger. In blaming, the attention gets shifted from 'Self' onto others. It is an easy way out, with no learning. Your purpose here is to learn about your Self and not about others. Shifted focus is going without, ignoring within. This shows lack of honesty, respect and betrayal of Self. You are not practising the teachings and are losing the balance. Once you lose the balance, you lose everything. Absolutely no lesson is learned in that area. If you make a choice to learn and accept, then the lesson will be learned in that area, field or category.*"

An injured ego may take the form of pain, frustration and feelings of helplessness. Because anger is a secondary reaction to the ego's hurt, we cannot work with it as a single entity. Childhood or past issues must be analyzed, understood, accepted, forgiven, healed, cleansed by the angels and then released. We have to return to the same incident many times in order to complete all levels of healing. The degree of levels that are healed depends upon the level of acceptance we have achieved.

The balance of anger is forgiveness. It is not a matter of becoming angry, being judgmental and assigning blame; it is an opportunity to learn. Anger is always ours alone. It belongs solely to us because it is created by *our* ego, emotional issues and past patterns of behaviour. Venting anger does not bring resolution; it merely temporarily satisfies the ego. At the same time, actions create earned consequences. Absolutely nothing happens without a purpose. Lessons are constantly given, with the same emotions resurfacing each time. If we do not learn life's lessons completely on all levels, this pattern will continue throughout our entire lives and could also be handed down to our children.

The White Angel said, "*Forgiveness and release from the emotional issues are not given, they have to be earned. Forgiveness only comes in the heart when we are in total and absolute acceptance of our anger, ego and the childhood incidents.*"

Levels of anger can be healed only when total and absolute focus remains on our-Self. We need to examine our issues by analyzing our emotional reactions to the lesson presented. We should not be concerned about what others are doing to us. People around us act the way they do because of their own issues. It is their journey and their problem to deal with – not ours to judge or correct them. Often we more readily see faults in others and form judgments rather than look at our own faults, actions and reactions so that we might learn and heal.

We act out our anger in two ways: either in an active or passive manner. Both reactions result in a negative situation. For example, a feeling of helplessness creates irritation, irritation creates anger, anger creates blame, blame creates revenge and revenge creates negative, harsh words or fighting. This is an active manner of projecting our anger. In a passive manner, feelings of helplessness create deep sadness, sadness creates self-pity, self-pity creates depression and depression creates negativity, feelings of hopelessness and loneliness. When we accept and release our active anger, we may experience deep sadness and depression. Through this experience we learn not to see ourselves as 'victims' and learn to forgive ourselves so that we may forgive others. When you have released your personal anger and have healed and you find yourself in a situation where another individual is projecting his or her anger on you, you will no longer be affected by it. You will be able to speak your own truth without reacting emotionally, judgmentally or self-defensively.

Seven Stages of Anger

There are seven stages of anger, each requiring analysis and understanding so that healing may occur.

Stage 1

In this first stage, we feel overwhelmed by emotion and feel that someone else is causing all this suffering and heartache. The emotions weigh heavy on our chests crying out for release, but we feel powerless. We try to release them by confiding in those we call friends or family. Men tend to keep their feelings to themselves more than women and in doing so, they push their feelings aside in order to feel numb. We may get stuck in this stage or any stage for a long time – even life after life until the soul is ready to learn about the Self.

Stage 2

In the second stage, we come to the realization that we have discussed our feelings enough and nothing has changed, nor do we feel better. We then react in anger and blame the person, thing or situation that we think to be the cause of our pain. In some instances, we place the blame on any and everything around us. Anger becomes a raging fire in our heads that consumes positive feelings of soul and forges a path of negative, destructive behaviour that injures everyone in its wake. We thus hurt ourselves and others. In such a state of rage or "temporary insanity", anger has no conscience, no feelings and respect for no one.

Stage 3

During this stage, we assume responsibility for our anger. We realize something is amiss with *me. I* am the one who is angry. It is *my* problem. Otherwise by angelic grace, we hear and heed the whisper of the Self: "I am hurting inside, and that is why I am angry". We pause, reflect and assume responsibility for our anger. Our actions catch up with us, and we acceptingly face the consequences.

Stage 4

The fourth stage is a testing stage: a test of acceptance. This is the initial step in the process of healing. At this point, whenever an irritating situation arises and we start to feel angry, we recognize this as mere reaction and make the anger our own. This shifts the focus to one of ownership; we focus on our Self (positive and within) as opposed to an outside force (negative). In doing so, we begin analyzing our feelings: "Why am I reacting to this situation? What is it that is hurting me so much? What do I really feel inside? Are these feelings new to me, or have they been present since I was a child?" You will find that these feelings are a result of the lesson presented by the situation and are not new to you.

The Blue Angel reminds us: "*Resentment and anger often come from childhood experiences; anger is your own pernicious habit.*"

Stage 5

We reach stage five when we recognize the particular childhood experience that is related to the present situation or experience. When we make this connection, sometimes the angels will heal us automatically to 'earn' this level. As if Pandora's box were opened, every suppressed emotion appear. Usually feelings of helplessness, powerlessness and frustration are accompanied by anger. As these old wounds are re-opened, we once again feel hurt, pain and suffering. We often cry in the same manner as we did as children. If we do not cry, it is because, as children, we were told that we must not cry. We cry because we feel sorry for ourselves, and we attempt to soothe our pain. This is a stage of enduring the lesson physically. At this point, we may direct our anger at our parents or some other perpetrator. Rather than becoming angry, we should be searching within so that we learn to *know* our Self and thereby know truth. It is not by the hands of a parent that this anger is created; it is by our choices and decisions.

Stage 6

Stage six is a decision-making stage. At this stage, we dispense with tears and self-pity because we know the real cause of our issue or pain. It is time for apologies and asking forgiveness of those individuals involved and the angels. It is also time to forgive ourselves. Forgiveness can be achieved on the inner levels; it does not have to be delivered in person (in physical form). We reach yet another level in acceptance and continue to the final step in healing anger on all seven levels.

Stage 7

At this stage, we become calm in our anger but still overwhelmed by the emotions. It is time to work on our issues by writing them down and working on each emotion individually. We begin to reflect on the number of times these same wounds have occurred and were re-opened in our lifetime. The process of healing is long as our understanding must reach the level of total and absolute acceptance of the Self.

The Blue Angel said, "*You cannot undermine our work and teachings by wanting quick fixes or instant gratification. Patience, perseverance and tolerance will pull you through all levels of healing the original issue in order to reach balance and wholeness by freeing the Self.*"

Give It to the Angels

When I was taught the seven stages of anger, I learned to release my pain. Whenever I was overwhelmed by my emotions and did not know what to do, where to begin, where to look or what I was looking for, I would become confused. I would begin with the help of the angel's prayer described in Chapter One. I was told "*Give it to us.*" I asked, "I should hand over the issue without working on it?" The Angel replied, "*Yes.*" Therefore I would request the angels to bubble the emotions; bind them in cords of divine light; cast them out and fill all vacant spaces with Divine Light. The issues were cleansed, released and thanks were given to the angels.

I realized that by giving an issue or emotion over to the angels, we open ourselves up to receiving their help. When we are in a receptive state, the angels are able to clear our minds so we become open, cleansed and clear to see the next step in our spiritual growth or the learning process. If we keep issues or emotions to ourselves, we remain closed to angelic assistance and are unable to move on towards the next step in healing. Using this method, I was able to heal one emotional issue at a time, for example, feelings of helplessness, self-pity, depression or anxiety, etc. Thankfully, the Blue Angel lovingly offered, "*Give all your concerns and worries to us.*"

Acceptance and Forgiveness

The White Angel said, "*Acceptance and forgiveness bring about the balance, humility and clarity of truth. Acceptance is a given factor in life; if you cannot accept your Self* [soul], *you cannot accept our teachings. Like yourself and know yourself.*"

Total acceptance and absolute understanding of life's experiences bring about forgiveness. Forgiveness cannot enter our hearts until we completely accept our anger, ego and emotional issues. This occurs when we no longer blame or judge. We must forgive ourselves so we can accept our Self. If we cannot forgive ourselves, we may be unknowingly judging ourselves. I found myself in a situation where, when I stopped judging and blaming others, I began to judge and blame myself. I needed to work through this issue because if I could not forgive myself, I could not possibly forgive others. Forgiveness of Self, involves making peace with *our* soul as well as with others.

The Golden Angel said, "*Freedom of Self comes from acceptance of Self. Acceptance of Self comes from accepting our stains, ignorance and mistakes.*"

Acceptance of Self, means that we completely accept everyone, everything and every situation in life. We recognize life's experiences as opportunities to learn about our Self. This change in attitude changes every situation from negative to positive. We do not forgive simply for forgiveness sake but rather so we learn humility, freedom of Self, love for Self and others. We also learn to forgive ourselves for suffering in ignorance. Acceptance leads directly to forgiveness

Lessons in Acceptance of My Ego and Anger

Many times, I was given lessons on anger and ego through my dreams, visions or pictures and incidents taking place in my daily life. Although I was shown in so many ways, I still had great difficulty in grasping the meaning of acceptance. I thought that as long my anger was justified – everyone gets angry once in a while – it was okay to be angry. I now realize my justification came from familial and inherited, social beliefs: a belief that it is correct and proper to be angry when someone makes a mistake. I could not see the matter through the eyes of angelic wisdom. The Golden Angel said, "*A lesson is coming.*"

I replied, "The lessons you give me are hard and not easy to understand." He replied *"Lessons are hard and a big struggle; if they weren't, one would not be where you are at the point of learning and accepting. Human ignorance makes it hard to perceive the truth and practice it. Nothing is given; it has to be earned. Recognize it and apply it."*

I discovered that anger is a signal to look within to discover answers. I found myself denying that I was angry; obviously I was not angry while I was talking to the angels. By refusing to accept my stains and lessons, I denied feelings of anger: I don't think I am angry." The Blue Angel gently asked "*Are you challenging us?*" This made me stop and consider what they were asking. I began to ponder what I had just said. I realized that they were referring to my anger. When I am angry, things matter, when I am not, they do not. I then understood what they had meant by telling me previously that humans suffer because of their ignorance. Therefore, I responded, "No." The Angel said, "*Either you are to listen and learn, or if you know everything then why ask? The human suffers because of ignorance and non-acceptance, which comes from human ego. Wise people are humble enough to accept.*"

I responded to the angelic teachings emotionally and egotistically. I learned to accept very slowly. It took me almost a year to accept my anger and ego, and it was just the first step and level in self-acceptance. All of this time, the angels were patiently and persistently showing me the same issue.

The Blue Angel said, "*When you respond* [react] *with emotions, your ego is making you arrogant and ignorant. The answers come from the surface, which means learned behaviour that comes from others, not from within. Feel deeper into your heart while you speak. Put your heart where your mouth is, only then your true hurt feelings of that little girl will surface.*"

At this point, I arrived at the second stage of anger. The White Angel reminded me, "*You were angry and fighting.*" I had been engaged in an argument the previous night. I responded to old wounds that were opened up by souls around me. I reacted in a judgmental manner by reminding them of their previous mistakes and of the pain they had caused me. I did not realize they were a catalyst to re-opening my old wounds so that I might be healed. As humans do, I chose to blame rather than do some serious soul-searching. I should have searched for the original cause of my anger: latent childhood. I received further clarification from the Blue Angel: "*Arguments are the justification of your ego or supporting your ego to be heard. It is a power struggle.*"

The White Angel elaborated further: "*You are looking for 'freedom of Self'. You are beating your head against the wall, feeling unworthy of self-love, self-respect, self-acceptance and happiness.*" This was entirely true. I was so unhappy that I began to blame my marriage and cried over my misfortune. My anger created so much negativity that it erased all positive thought-forms of my Self. Thankfully, the White Angel enlightened me: "*You were crying over useless thought-forms, which was a waste of time. You are running away from Self. Love can start from your side by sharing love in different manners through kindness, saying a kind word, an act of kindness with empathy, without judging, just listening to others and making them feel important.*"

I told the angels that I needed to learn about self-love, self-trust, faith in self, self-respect, self-belief, self-worth and self-reliance. I felt I also needed the discipline not to choose anger and ego over my Self. The White Angel replied: "*All of this will automatically be there once you learn total and absolute acceptance of Self. Forgive, accept, release, let go and free yourself to gain freedom of Self.*"

Although I was willing to accept my anger, I still had questions. I was shown a moment from my childhood when my father was angry with me. I asked, "How can I forgive and let go when I still feel pain and hurt? How can I love and respect when I have none in return?" My struggle was great, and I found it very difficult to move on. I was also tired and could not see a way out.

The White Angel said, "*So this is what you think and you have let it take over you; or you can bubble it and cast it away and be who you are. Do not let negative choices take over you. Take your stand, get hold of yourself, make your decision and learn to be a little more flexible by giving room to positive thinking. Don't you want to experience true love in your life? Cultivate your own unconditional love by total 'acceptance of Self' without any judgments, irritations, blaming and lack of Self.*"

I struggled with the nature of learning: its difficulty and the amount of time required. For me, the hard-earned results came through persistently learning – although it was very difficult at times – and being tested by the angels. I soon realized that answers are not directly and supernaturally given; they must be earned through personal work on the Self to fully understand the experience and recognize truth. These truths were all new to me when I began my spiritual journey. I tried to resolve my anger and could not. I prayed and offered it to the angels, but they refused it. Instead, my issues were symbolically shown to me: I was given a vision of little girl carrying a wagon filled with stones. I knew the stones represented my negativity, but I could not connect them to the real issue.

The Blue Angel said, "*Leave other people alone. Stop interfering with them by showing their stains and issues. They can only recognize them if they are looking for their ego. If you focus on yourself as much as you are focussing on them, you will be much better off clearing your wagon. You exercise no self-control; your anger is like a tidal wave – it comes in strong and goes away. You needed to learn acceptance, humility, gratitude and respect for Self, God and others.*" The Golden Angel added: "*You are in a mood of gloom and doom, trying to soothe your wounds by emotional clutches, feeling sorry for yourself and not working on your wagon.*"

The Blue Angel threw more stones in the wagon and said, "*You seek instant results and are avoiding the real issues by running away from Self. You are not practising the teachings unless something is instantly gained. You don't want to earn it. You have no commitment, no trust, no faith, no sincerity whatsoever.*" The White Angel added" *You are hiding behind your emotions.*" The Blue Angel continued: "*Learn, learn, learn. The spiritual journey is acceptance and learning. Without learning, the journey is empty. You are not consistent in looking for your answers. You are not following the teachings.*"

I prayed and asked forgiveness for my mistakes and ignorance then made a conscious decision to focus always on myself and not on others, no matter how greatly the actions of others affected me. I realized that by placing blame on others, I chose to see myself as a victim. I began to connect with the little girl's pain, helplessness, ego and anger. I understood that these feelings were mine in the first place and were created by my own hands. My inner child attracted the situation so that my heart and soul might receive healing.

The Angel of Knowledge, the Golden Angel, came to me to offer answers that I had been diligently seeking but was far from finding. I was shown that I had been carrying a blanket around my shoulders for the past few days. I incorrectly assumed the blanket represented protection or preservation. The Golden Angel corrected: "*The blanket represents your imbalance. You have put it on in order to preserve your ego. You have gone overboard to negative thoughts by being defensive and judgmental and have therefore lost your balance.*"

This was the first time I really understood the meaning of judgment and realized how far ego goes to judge others. I justified blame by thinking I had the right to defend myself. The ego, being very insecure, becomes extremely defensive. I then realized that self-defence was unnecessary. I simply needed to focus on my Self and accept responsibility for my reactions and issues. It became clear that I should be bothered by absolutely nothing. When I re-shifted my focus, my real issues were worked out.

The Blue Angel said, "*Shifted focus changes the perspective. When you change your perspective* [from positive self to negative self], *you lose your balance. When you lose your balance, you have lost everything.*"

The Golden Angel added: "*The stones in the wagon were your stumbling steps as your focus was shifted from within to without* [from positive to negative]." I realized the truth of this statement. So many times I had stumbled, but when I was shown the way, I regained control, corrected my error and learned. As I mentioned before, it certainly was not easy; often I felt lonely, depressed and lacking in everything. When I asked about my depression, the angel said, "*Depression is the price you pay when you don't look and work on your issues and feel sorry for yourself. Depression also comes from feeling lack of power of Self.*"

The Golden Angel then told me: "*A change and a move are coming. Change in consciousness brings about relief from distress. To gladden is to lighten you. You will be moving to the next level, which will be on all phases or on all levels. This will be a move from gloom and doom. Continue with your prayers, writing and future travels.*"

Conclusion

Usually we are unable to see our own stains because we are conditioned to live in an environment where ego is more commonly used rather than recognized for what it truly is, the false Self. For example, once when speaking to a lady, I was asked what my book was about. I responded that it deals with healing emotional issues with the help of the angels. She asked, "What kind of issues?" I replied, "Can you think of anything or anyone in your life that bothers you?" At first she said, "No" but then said, "Just this friend of ours who constantly talks about himself and never gives us a chance to talk about ourselves. He never asks us how we are doing. This makes me feel very irritated, and I dislike him." I asked her if it made her feel angry. When she responded positively, I asked, "What do you feel prior to the irritated feelings?" She started to think but was unsure. I then asked if this situation made her feel helpless, being in a situation where she was not allowed to speak but only listen. "Well, yes", she admitted. I then asked if she thought these feelings were hers alone and that her friend was not affected in any way. I explained, The feelings will remain with you even when you leave your friend. Your friend is creating a situation arranged by the angels to resurface your emotions so you can heal the issue." She agreed. I continued, "Then why judge your friend, when he is doing you a favour?" She said, "Oh boy, you gave me a lot to think about. I had never thought of looking at it in this manner." I was able to offer this advice because of the Blue Angel's teaching: "*If you analyze everything in life, about life, ask, seek and you will find the answers within.*"

Knowing the truth about our stains and accepting them is one thing; being willing to work on them in order to realize the truth is entirely another. The angels made certain that I always practised the lessons I was told to learn. I learned that there are many levels or steps to our growth towards acceptance before we reach the point of complete and absolute acceptance of Self.

No life is easy, nor will it ever be. But it can become easier if we view experiences from the soul's or Higher Self's perspective. Humans can only move beyond their ego if they consciously choose to do so. Regardless of one's lifespan, every person, at one time or another, encounters heartache, suffering, grief, anguish, hardship or heartbreak – to name but a few of life's trials. Life lessons are presented by trial. How we choose to react determines the quality of our lives. We believe what we choose to believe. We can either accept life's lessons or reject them. We either claim ownership of our issues or exact blame and judgment. The choice remains ours for lessons are given to all.

If you recognize any awakening, thanks and gratitude belong to the angels.
Thank you, angels, for your wisdom and knowledge.

6

Process of Healing Emotional Issues

Please protect, bless and cleanse the following chapter. Thank you.

LIFE IS A CONTINUOUS process of lessons, tests and learning. The lessons are basically created by emotional patterns that are set in early childhood. Our actions and reactions further complicate these issues. The outer pain, such as the loss of a loved one or a pet, divorce, severed relationships, accidents, illness, simple day-to-day living or struggle is merely the projection of our inner pain. We carry these wounds within us for a very long time. Life's situations or experiences are mirror reflections of our inner state, which in turn open latent wounds.

To recognize this, we must focus on our childhood traumas and search well within our hearts, minds and souls for the connection to the present situation. All answers reside within. Some of us may not have early childhood memories, but can seek angelic assistance. Those of us who do easily recall childhood memories find them to be the source of our emotional reactions and behaviour. When you find the answers, you are often struck by how obvious they are. It is like using common sense to look in common places for answers.

The search becomes our journey to find the truth within the Self. This spiritual journey will enable us to deal effectively with our issues and problems. The angels showed me two main sources of emotional issues and patterns.

The first is our parental, handed-down habits, behaviour, emotional issues, patterns and beliefs. We often find ourselves behaving like our parents and have no idea how to stop this behaviour. When I recognized this, the angel gave me the healing process and procedure to resolve these parental issues. The healing process is described later in this chapter.

The second source of our patterns and issues is childhood trauma or the way we react to a situation created by a harsh experience in our childhood. This experience creates our journey of emotional issues and patterns. There can be a third source of patterns and issues: our past-life or lives' traumatic death and issues that are carried forward in our soul as karmic patterns (blueprints) to be resolved in this lifetime so that our soul may be freed from the necessity of repeating the same issues life after life. This was very evident in my case, where I could not rid myself of recurring throat infections.

Our current personality is the result of past, unresolved emotional issues and patterns and the choices we have made. We cannot simply leave the past behind. We must accept, learn and heal the past; otherwise, the present and future will be a continual representation of these unresolved issues. The issues, presented as lessons, include the same circumstances and emotions; only the play is altered. The lessons may now involve different people, different situations, different places and different forms, such as physical illnesses or physical pain. In angel's words " *The act remains the same only the play gets altered.*"

Memories of my earliest childhood incident resurfaced when the angels were teaching me about anger and ego. This incident occurred when I was about seven years old. It was a day of Dewali Pooja, a Hindu religious festival. All of our family had gathered to pray. My mother had prepared sweets as offerings to the God and Goddess. We were allowed to eat the sweets but only after prayer. There were also a lot of sugar pieces, called Batashas, for prayers. I ate one, and my father saw me chewing. He suspected that I had eaten the prepared sweet. He repeatedly asked what I was eating, and I told him the truth: I was eating a piece of sugar, not the sweet offering for the God.

He did not believe me and became very angry, accusing me of lying. His anger turned into rage. I could see that his face was turning red, and that he was ready to strike me. By this time, I was crying hysterically, in total fear and helplessness. I did not know what to say. My mother intervened by pulling me away from him and telling him not to ruin his mood for a trivial incident like this at the time of prayer.

This ordeal left me with emotional scars such as fear, helplessness and a desperation to free myself from the situation. I felt humiliated and frustrated – sad and hurt that no one believed me. Ultimately, I felt unloved. This was only a repetition of preexisting issues, but I did not know this at the time. As an adult, I could see the same emotional patterns repeating throughout my life through different incidents and different people. I also noticed that as I was getting older, the issues were becoming worse. I worked on these inherited issues and habits for almost two years. During this time, I began to realize that a lot of my mother's habits were incorporated into my own personality. I also recognized a few of my father's.

I asked the angels to show me how to work on these habits so that they might be healed and removed from me.

The Blue Angel said, "*Give the habits and issues back to the original owner. They were not yours in the first place.*"

The Creator advised: "*You must look at your mother and father at soul level while working on parental handed-down issues. Keep your head above the emotions because they will try to drag you down. Also know that each individual is on its own journey.*" This means that while you have chosen to learn the truth about yourself, it does not mean that your parents or other people are on this same path. Your teachings are specifically for *you* and passing information to others is not always helpful. Looking at parents on a soul level means that you are not looking to find faults or blaming them in any manner, you simply want to be free from it and move on. There is a process and procedure for healing these latent emotional scars.

The Process and Procedure of Healing

- Recognize the patterns, issues and habits and to whom they belong.
- Invoke the angels through part one of the prayer in Chapter Two. Bubble the parents or parties involved by asking the angels to encircle them with Divine Light. You can calmly discuss what you are undertaking with the help of the angels with your parents. Discuss things peacefully

and unemotionally.

- Request the angels to bring you back to the time in your childhood when these habits and issues were absorbed by you (usually from birth to three years of age). Help the child to put them, one by one, into an imaginary bag. Give it back to the parent (the original owner) by placing the bag in his or her circle with the help of the angel.
- Request the angels to cut all emotional bonds to these issues or habits. Ask that all ties be bound in cords of Divine Light where none shall escape and that they be cast into love and light. Have the angels fill the spaces in the child's heart with Divine Light. This is the first part of the prayer contained in the second chapter of this book.
- Ask for the angels' forgiveness for everyone by first forgiving yourself and then your parents. Realize that your parents behaved in the best way they knew how or because of their own inherited issues.
- Request the angels to heal the child's heart on all levels by bringing that child into your heart and allowing him or her to become one with you.
- Cleanse and release all parties or parents, including yourself, in the Divine Light of the Creator. Give thanks to the angels and God.
- A variation: to heal a childhood trauma that does not involve parents, simply mentally return to the incident and heal the issue as above. If you cannot find answers and feel a strong pull towards feelings and emotions, or if you recognize that the source may come from elsewhere (your soul may make you aware of this), then these issues may belong to a past life. You can ask the angels to bring

you back in time where these specific emotional traumas originated. Then request healing as described in the above paragraphs.

The nature of emotional issues, on the first four levels, are described in the succeeding paragraphs. We must examine these levels so we can understand how we are affected by our emotions. We need to know how to heal them so that we may know our Self.

The Physical Level: These are incidents that take place in our everyday life (at home or at work) and involve family members, other people, pets, things we dislike, social, cultural or religious beliefs, handed-down habits, patterns and issues. Imbalance on this level causes illness. On this level, physical illness can be a past-life issue or a violent death manifested as *dis-ease* in this life-time.

The Emotional Level: Childhood trauma, scars, experiences of pain and suffering, hardship, heartache, fear, guilt, lack of self-love, lack of self-worth, lack of self-respect, feelings of emptiness, etc. all occur on the emotional level. On this level we work on the heart's issues to free our Self. The soul feels trapped, and we need to feel joy on the physical level. Imbalance on this level causes dependency or attachments.

The Mental Level: On this level, we know the difference between the Self and ego – the soul and heart. We realize that we have the freedom to choose how we react, whether it be emotionally (through the heart) or spiritually (through the soul). From this realization, we focus our attention on the Self so that we may recognize and heal the issue. We acknowledge the choices of focussing on Self (positive) or shifting the focus onto others (negative). We become aware of balance and imbalance and the consequences of negative or positive choice. Imbalance on this level causes ignorance.

The Spiritual Level: Throughout the healing process, the angels are always with us and assist through our thought-forms. Acknowledge the angelic presence, guidance and healing. Have faith, trust, and belief in Self and in the angels. Imbalance on this level causes psychosis.

The Blue Angel said, *"As long as these levels are not in balance, you won't achieve your purpose in life. The purpose in life is to learn and know about your Self and no one else. This happens through lessons in learning so that you can achieve balance and wholeness."*

❁ ❁ ❁

Over a two-year period, as I worked on my habits and issues, healing was achieved on a certain level. The level of healing equalled my level of acceptance of my anger and ego. For a short time, my anger was shifted to my father, which did not help me to learn or to keep my balance. The Blue Angel reminded me: *"Rekha, you can't sit on a fence any longer. Time is now and running out if you don't do something about yourself. Either you make it or lose it. Anger should not be there for anyone at any given time. If it exists, it is all yours. You are not going deep enough to find the answers. Why don't you admit that you are angry and ask for forgiveness? Wise people live in humble acceptance."* The White Angel said, *"You will have to find a way to forgive and release your father."*

I wondered where else I should look and if I should search

deeper. And if so, how much deeper did I need to go? I prayed for help and answers. Once again, a childhood issue came to mind. As before, I could not quite connect it to my issues and questions at that time. My level of understanding was not developed to a point where I could see and understand as I do now.

Then, in August 1996, our budgie, who was my daughter's trained, lovable, intelligent pet, became sick. I decided to take the bird outside for fresh air and sunlight. At first, I just took her outside for a little while. I brought her back inside the house with me while I attended to some unfinished business. I opened the cage door while we were in the house. When I finished my work we went outside again but I completely forgot about the cage door being open. I sat down on a chair and placed the birdcage on another chair – completely unaware that the cage door was open. It was as if the thought had been erased from my mind. I sat looking at the bird. She knew the cage door was open. She looked at me, looked at the door, hopped down to her lower perch and soared out the door, high in the pale blue sky. The first words that flew out of my mouth were: "Oh my God, what have I done? I cannot lose this bird. It is not mine. How am I going to tell my daughter what I have done to her bird?" I was devastated. I began to cry. Feeling hurt and blaming myself, I wondered how I could do such a foolish thing. I cried to the angels, "Why did I do this?" and I heard the Blue Angel say: *"It wasn't done by your hands. It was done by our hands to teach you your lesson."*

At this stage, I knew enough to apply the angels' teachings. My pain was so great it felt as if I had lost one of my own children. During the next few days I monitored my emotions in this situation. I felt sad for the lost bird, thinking "that poor baby is alone, looking for our home to come back to but is lost and cannot find it. She must be dying with hunger, thirst, and exhaustion from flying. If not, the cooler, Canadian August nights will kill her for sure." I felt sad, depressed and spent a lot of time crying for I was certain she was dead.

All of a sudden, I realized that I was not feeling these emotions for the bird! The outer pain was merely a reflection of *my* inner state. All of these feelings were for myself I now saw myself in this same situation but in an early childhood incident that I had already been made aware of.

This incident occurred when I was about four years old. To escape the summer heat, our family was vacationing in India's hill station. My parents had rented a house singularly situated on a high, hilly top surrounded by the forest. On this particular morning, my mother bathed and dressed me, and then she began bathing my sisters. I came out of the house, took my little cane, and set out towards the forest. I walked quite far in the forest without realizing what I was doing. Quite some time passed before I began trying to find my way back to the house.

Every direction seemed the same. I did not know the direction from which I had entered the forest. I tried to find my way back but was hopelessly lost. The more I tried, the more confused I became. I was frightened and started crying hysterically. Of course, no one could hear me. I knew I could not find my way out, but I kept on walking and crying for a long time because I desperately wanted to get back home.

I was exhausted from crying and walking, hungry and thirsty. Eventually, I felt I could not go on any longer so I gave up and sat down to die. All I remember was falling asleep and what took place after that, only the angels know.[12] I did not even remember the reunion with my family. Sometime later my mother told me that an old, fair-skinned man, with a white beard and dressed in a white robe, brought me home that evening. She added, "We were looking for you all day. When he brought you home, we were very happy. The man vanished without giving us a chance to thank him." He could not have possibly walked down the hill that quickly, so we set out to look for him. Nobody thought much of this incident, including myself, but now I know that an angel in human form brought me back.

This incident is the one that set my soul's learning journey in motion for this life-time. This incident created all my emotional issues and patterns. I gave my "power of Self" to my negative choices as I gave up within my Self. This was my karmic pattern set forth in this life from where I was to begin my journey of learning. All souls have their own patterns set in different ways because no two journeys are alike. We are all here for the same purpose, however, and that is to learn about our Self.

With this new understanding I knew that I needed to work with the little girl's wounded heart and pray for healing of the emotional trauma. I also wanted the lost budgie to return. Using the process and procedure described in this chapter, I began to heal my emotional issues one at a time, as I started to recognize them. As I was working through my issues, I heard the Blue Angel promise: *"Your bird will be returned once you learn your lesson."* I wanted to believe this, but I also knew that the angels test us even harder when we are sifting through our

12 I now realize that this was a scenario from a past-life death. It was played out in my childhood to be healed in this life-time. I requested healing for the past life as well.

emotional garbage. I wondered if these thoughts of the budgie returning were my own wishful thinking, so I told my daughter about it. She told me she had had a dream of the bird returning home and playing with her. I then realized that if the bird were to return home, I must do my part in helping her return.

I continued to work on my issues, and at the same time placed an advertisement in the community paper for the lost, blue budgie. After a week I received a call. I went to see the bird, but it wasn't ours; this was a male budgie. The individual who found it, did not want it so I brought him home saying that if the original owner were found, I would be happy to return the bird. I had little hope of finding our budgie, but I ran my advertisement for another week. At the end of the week, a phone call came while I was at work. My son answered and as the caller described the bird's imitation of human voices, he recognized our budgie instantly. The children brought her home the next day. She recognized us and began kissing us, but I could see that she had changed. The lady said that when she found the bird, she couldn't even fly four feet high. She had found our bird on her driveway, the evening after she flew away. This bird had flown quite far. It was quite an ordeal to survive one chilly night and two whole days without food.

As I prayed for my healing, I automatically prayed for the bird's healing as well. What I felt for myself, I also felt for our budgie. I thanked the angels for the lesson, healing and blessings. By this time I had developed a self-testing method for assessing the level of healing I had reached. I knew that in a balanced state of consciousness an individual feels neither happy nor sad, nor reacts emotionally to any situation. Whenever I felt my emotions surfacing while I was watching something sad on the television or reading in my journal of past hurt and pain, I would recognize that the healing had not been achieved on its last level. If I felt unaffected by certain issues, I knew that I no longer needed to work in that area.

The Blue Angel said, *"What you have learned and can learn at any given time is a degree (level) of what you are familiar with, to understand and accept your stains and emotional issues. This means that you may heal your issue at one point in your life, but it may not be resolved at its last level. You will have to revisit this issue later on in life when your understanding and acceptance have grown. The teachings are not complete without an experience of a lesson being presented, and it must be recognized and understood. You must physically experience the endurance of the lesson and heal the heart's issues in order to free the Self."*

The White Angel added: *"Once you are given the insight to recognize your issue, we will always test you to see whether you have learned to get over the issue or not."* As I mentioned before I often found the angels' teachings and tests difficult. To adopt their teachings, I had to work very hard on myself with total commitment, trust and belief. The angels are extremely adamant about lessons being learned. We cannot move forward unless we understand the full meaning of the lessons being presented and are healed on the last level.

In 1997, I moved to the United States to join my husband. Our children decided to stay in Canada. I found myself in a new place, with no friends, no children and a busy husband who spent long hours at work. I felt extremely lonely. All my patterns of lack of Self and emotional issues began to re-appear intensely. I revisited feelings of a lack of Self: self-love, self-trust, self-worth, self-esteem, self-determination, self-respect, faith and self-belief. The related emotional issues were feelings of sadness, helplessness, abandonment, fear and depression. I felt unloved, unwanted and desperate to get out of this situation. I felt I had nothing to look forward to and felt trapped.

These were the same old, tired issues of the little girl. While driving around in the new city, I got lost many times. I was always afraid of getting lost. I had no sense of direction. To make matters worse, my car's battery would lose power while I drove on the streets and highway, causing my engine to stall. I saw this as a reflection of my inner feelings of death and dying. I tried to cure my loneliness by finding a job, but nothing could ease my heartache. I prayed constantly for healing, but it could only work to the extent that I had accepted my emotional conditions and physical surroundings.

Sometimes I would accept the situation that had been presented to me, but the next minute, I was back to feeling sorry for myself and assigning blame and passing judgment. I refer to this as "the tidal wave stage," in which I kept saying to myself that all of this is happening because I was creating it, and I have to learn to accept it. Thinking in this manner, I regained strength, but the sea of emotions was so deep that I found myself constantly being pulled underneath its current. I caught myself looking for answers outside of myself, which resulted in nothing but blame and judgment.

This deep sea of emotions is described in Hindu scriptures as *Bhav-Sagar* or *Bhavnow Ka Sugar*. After crossing this deep sea of emotions, the freedom of Self, or *Moksha*, waits for you on the opposite shore. Many drown in this sea. Those who make it, succeed only because of the angels' healing. The Creator cautioned me: *"Keep your head above the emotions, and don't let them drag you down."*

During this testing period, I found it very difficult to maintain focus on my Self. I did not fully comprehend the lesson being taught. Also, I had not achieved the level of total and absolute acceptance of my Self. My emotional pain, compounded by the death of our budgie, left me totally heartbroken. The day she died, I was very busy and paid her little attention. In the evening when I called to her, she gathered up her last bit of strength and came to me. It was too late to do anything for her; I knew she was dying. My husband held her in his hands for a while, then I took her in my hands and prayed to the angels to take care of her soul. She looked at me as I kissed her and told her that she would be all right. She kissed me once and a few minutes later she left with the angels. This is the way the angels had planned her journey. I knew that there were more lessons to be learned from this soul's departure.

For the next few days, I shed many pain-filled tears at the loss of my beloved pet. I had often felt that she was the only soul that truly loved me. Although she could no longer continue to return the kisses I gave her, I knew she loved me deeply as well. If her love had not been so great, I would not be missing her so very much. I wanted to put this mortally-attached love to rest because it was too painful. I feel the angels made good use of this soul to teach me many lessons. Back in 1994, this same bird was dying. She seemed to worsen with each day, but after a week of prayers for her healing, she fully recovered. The angels brought her back to life and completely healed her. I felt this was their way of showing me how I was brought back to life when I was lost and feared dying in the forest.

Lesson of Human Attached Love

My lack of self-love created a strong need for human love from my little bird. I did not realize how emotionally attached I was to her until the time came to give her up. The angels showed me that by loving this soul from my heart's desire, I had attached my soul to her soul with emotional cords. Neither of us could move forward until I released this human love and let go of her.

I prayed to the angels to dissolve these cords of humanly attached love by casting them away, filling the empty spaces and conditioning my heart and mind with God's unconditional love and light. I requested healing for both of us by cleansing and releasing all into the care of the Creator's Divine Light. I thanked the angels for their wisdom and healing.

Human love is temporary and sometimes short-lived. It eventually causes us pain, but teaches us to look within for the true love of Self and to cultivate within our Self the unconditional love of God. The ego in our heart will always desire to look outside of us into the physical world and will not allow us to look into our Soul or God's world. With unconditional love, we still love the same but without attachment, hurt and grief. God and the angels do not have humanly attached love for us. They have unconditional love for all souls. Experiencing the unconditional love of God is warm, soft, gentle and immensely fulfilling. It is a feeling that brings no more desire for anything in the world except for this type of love. It feels light, soft and peaceful – as if you are floating in it.

These experiences showed me what I needed to learn about humanly attached love. I first needed to experience the unconditional love of God. Then, and only then, could I experience human love without the extreme heartbreak and attachments. To know the truth of my soul, I had to seek truth, knowledge and understanding by applying the angels' wisdom through their teachings about my life's experiences.

Lesson of My Guilt

Of course, guilt is never instantaneously erased. I carried guilt over the death of our budgie because I did not pay enough attention to her on the day she died. I thought that maybe she could have been saved if I had noticed her weakness earlier. The angel said, *"All souls are alone in their journey of enduring the lesson."* I understood that I couldn't possibly be able to share her pain and suffering. I accepted that all occurrences are planned the way they are by Soul's karmic issues and patterns. I was not allowed to interfere in her suffering or in enduring her lesson. This is why I was kept away from her. With this understanding, I was able to release my guilt.

Lesson of Enduring the Experience

Lessons are firstly presented by being shown a past incident or circumstance. It must be physically endured in order to learn and understand about our Self. If a soul chooses to learn, endurance of pain, hurt, suffering, illness, heartache and hardship can be a great teacher. Endurance teaches humility and acceptance, which culminates in soul-searching from where we find our answers. Our daily prayers bring about healing by the angels when a lesson is being learned by endurance. The Angel said: *"Healing is not a given factor – it must be earned."*

Sometimes the length of the period of endurance seems unbearable, but mortals have no choice if they want to learn the lesson being presented. During such a period I asked the angels, "How long will I have to go on like this?" The Blue Angel replied, *"Perseverance will pull you through. The teachings are not complete without an experience of a lesson, endurance of the lesson, understanding of the lesson, healing the heart's pain, and issues to free the Self. In this lesson of tolerance, patience, courtesy, respect and humility are all in one package."*

No matter what hardship I suffered, I always knew that the angels were teaching me something about my Self, although I was unaware of what this something might be at the time. I knew a certain period of endurance was required to learn a lesson. I also knew that if I kept searching for answers and kept resolving the issues with perseverance, I would overcome the hardship. The Blue Angel said, *"You must have one hundred percent commitment, total trust, faith, devotion, respect and gratitude for what is given to you as a lesson and learn."*

It takes time to understand a lesson and learn from it. The angels look at the journey on a spiritual (soul) level, not on an emotional level. The angels and God do not have emotions and stains, nor does our soul. The angels understand human frailties. I often found that the angels stepped aside while I was playing the victimizing game of feeling sorry for myself and blaming and judging others. When I was ready to accept and learn, the angels provided answers and healing.

Reason for Being Alone and Feeling Lonely

Deep inside, all souls are lonely, empty, alone and sad because of a feeling of lack of God's light and love within the Self. In an attempt to fill this void, we keep ourselves busy with worldly activities, active social lives, family, friends, etc. Then, one day, circumstances intervene, and we are forced to look within. We find ourselves feeling lonely, alone and sad; this is how our lessons begin. The Blue Angel said, *"You are in denial that you were lonely and alone with your experience as a child; therefore, release it to us."* By releasing it, I understood that I needed to accept that I had feelings of loneliness and of being alone. As a result, I was lonely and felt alone all of my life and during my spiritual journey because this was meant to be a test of my endurance. The Angel asked, *"Are these feelings new to you?"*

I gave a negative reply because I could see emotions repeatedly resurfacing throughout my life, albeit with varying incidents. These feelings were set on the day I got lost in the forest and gave away the power of Self to my negative choices. These feelings existed when I was growing up, when I was a teenager, when I got married and when I was raising my children. The only difference was that my attention was diverted from my Self while I was busy taking care of my worldly responsibilities.

I was now at a point in my life where I realized that the same emotions resurfaced and would not go away unless I accepted, understood, resolved and healed them. I find it quite amazing that basic issues remain throughout our lives and remain unchanged. No matter how often we change our surroundings, change our partners or even change our careers, the emotional hardships are repeatedly presented to us until we face the lessons we need to learn.

At this point in my life, my heart was heavy with unresolved issues. I felt unsettled about anything and everything in life. I had no choice; I had to resolve my issues in order to move forward. Once while praying for healing, the angels showed me an experience related to the little girl's wounded heart. I was shown a mirror in the heart that reflected a lack of Self, my patterns and emotional issues. The mirror in the little girl's heart attracted the incidents according to her patterns and emotional issues. Consequently, this invited different people and situations throughout my later life to reopen my old wounds. My lack of Self, emotional issues and patterns created all of these situations. I realized that I had given the power of Self over to my ego, out of fear. This reflected a lack of self-trust and karmic patterns in my soul. It was created by my own doing, and it was my problem.

This understanding opened me up to an absolute acceptance of my Self. I completely assumed responsibility of my Self and for everything that had happened to me. I felt great sorrow and anguish for being angry and judgmental towards people who were chosen to be in my life so that I might learn. I became very grateful to the angels for presenting my lessons through the souls around me. I was ready to ask forgiveness of everyone and release my anger. I remembered the White Angel's words that I had to find a way to release my father. I prayed to the angels to help me release everyone.

I requested the angels to remove the mirrors of each emotion from my heart and soul in order to provide healing on the last level of my heart's issues. It took several months as each emotion surfaced in its own time. Healings were given daily. I thanked the angels for the healing and prayed that I would never have to repeat these experiences. After each healing, I found that my heart no longer ached. It was amazing to feel pain and suffering vanish instantly from my heart. The pain disappeared, yet I still felt lonely because my soul was not healed.

I understood why the White Angel said: *"Acceptance and forgiveness bring about the balance, humility and clarity of the truth. Learning about our emotions leads us to discovery of Self. Healing of the emotions leads to freedom of Self. The tests of the issues lead us to holiness and balance."* The Blue Angel said: *"Healing results in acceptance of Self-love. The purpose of healing is to become one with the angels, which is the soul's ultimate destiny* [in order] *to achieve balance and wholeness."*

Hardships are not quickly resolved. Understanding of Self comes slowly, but ultimately change and permanent healings occur. This requires applying the teachings with patience, tolerance and trust. Know that things will change when the lesson is learned and earned in the angel's time. I knew that I still had far to go.

Daily Affirmation for Loneliness

May the following affirmations help you come to the realization that you truly are a child of God and are unconditionally loved by the Creator. Use these affirmations daily so that you too may receive healing and come to a full realization of the Self – a Self that is never alone.

> I have the angels, God and myself with me in every moment of my life.
>
> I have absolute and total trust, faith and belief in the angels, God and myself.
>
> They are my providers, companions, helpers, teachers, healers and a guiding light in the direction I shall be moving in.
>
> The angels will bring everything together when the time is right. All occurrences take place in life in the angels' time.
>
> All my needs are provided for.
>
> The angels provide a fountain of plenitude and plethora in my life.

Thank you, angels, for providing for my needs – both learning and healing – and for your guidance throughout my life.

Lesson in Giving Power of Self to Negative Choices and Feeling a Lack of Self

When initial issues and patterns are set, every soul feels helpless and powerless. All of us were too young to do anything about it at the time; this is why later in life we become frustrated and angry with ourselves without knowing why. In our anger, we blame the present situation and people around us.

The Angel said, "*Self is empty without God's Light. Without Self there is no guidance or purpose in life. The power of Self comes from accepting God and all of the Self, such as self-trust, self-belief, self-respect, loyalty to the Self, and speaking the truth of the Self.*"

Lack of Self or non-acceptance of the Self creates insecurity. In this situation, the individual gives the power of Self to negative choices or to his or her dependencies. This results because of the lack of a center of grounding or lack of focus on the Self. We look outside ourselves and into the physical world for self-gratification, which only temporarily satisfies but never sates. The moment we experience self-doubt, we lose our focus and our center of grounding. When we doubt, fear creeps in and we lose our balance by giving the power of Self to our ego. Doubting means not only doubting the Self but also God and the angels.

The Golden Angel said, "*If you are not true to yourself, you cannot be true to others. If you don't accept yourself, you cannot accept God, the angels, or others. If you don't respect yourself, you cannot respect God, the angels' teachings or others. If you are not loyal to yourself, you cannot be loyal to the angels' teachings. If you do not believe and trust in yourself, you cannot believe in God, the angels or others. If you do not know yourself, how could you possibly know anyone else, except to judge them?*"

When we judge others by blaming, criticizing and faultfinding, we give our power of Self to our negative choices (ego). While we eventually discover retribution, we learn nothing about our Self. Our focus is shifted outwardly, onto others. We should be asking ourselves, "What do I have to learn about myself from this situation or incident?"

It is hard to comprehend the meaning of acceptance, because we learn to live by terms and conditions of the physical world.

These terms and conditions are negative and reactive. We are here to learn to find peace within and gain back the power of Self by freeing our soul from these emotional issues and negativity. Our soul yearns for God's love and light and its divine home. We can either focus on stains and emotions or focus on our Self. We cannot focus on both at the same time. Choices are made accordingly. We condition our mind, depending on what we want or desire.

Lack of Self

Lack of Self-Trust

When we do not trust in our Self, we give charge to others by trusting them. We will find that we are often taken advantage of, which in itself is another lesson. We tend to trust others rather than trusting our own instincts or feelings. We look to others for approval. If we trust in our Self, we learn to live in acceptance of our Self. I was told by the angels: "*In order to earn the trust of others, you must give the trust to your Self. Have trust in yourself, in the teachings and in your instincts. Feel it, know it and act upon it.*"

Lack of Self-Belief

When we believe in others yet do not believe in ourselves, there is a lack of self-belief. When we have the courage and faith to believe in our Self, we come to understand that everything in life has a purpose: that purpose is learning more about the Self. Believe in Self so that you may believe in God.

Lack of Faith in the Self

Lack of faith in our Self brings about a lack of belief and lack of trust. Without this belief, trust or faith, one cannot believe in God and the angels. Faith in Self should not be an empty faith. It should be a knowing faith that becomes our reality. By having faith, we know that God will provide for all of our needs. We are always given what we ask.

Lack of Self-Determination

Lack of self-determination causes a deficit of courage. We lose our commitment and give up on the Self; there is no devotion to Self. By having self-determination, you will always find what you seek.

Lack of Self-Reliance

A lack of self-reliance stems from a lack of knowledge, understanding, and confidence. One cannot make decisions and show initiative. With self-reliance, one knows, understands and chooses for the Self.

Lack of Self-Respect

We experience a lack of self-respect when we feel low, humiliated, hurt and angry at ourselves. We often feel betrayed and have little respect for anyone or anything, including ourselves. Self-respect fosters respect and acceptance for the Self, others, the angels, and God.

Lack of Self-Worth

Feelings of diminished self-worth leaves one feeling empty and disappointed, as if one were a failure, powerless, desperate and unworthy. The end result is low self-esteem. We often feel as if we cannot do anything right. Self-worth brings us to total and absolute acceptance of the Self and to knowledge of the power of the Self.

All of these issues were very personal to me and gratefully, I was lovingly and patiently taught by the angels: The Blue Angel said, "*Rekha, you must know what is worth doing, what you are doing, and what is your priority. Lack of self-esteem, non-acceptance of the Self and insecurities are making you give power of Self to the negative choices that you are making. It will lower your self-esteem even more. You must learn to stand in the light of your truth and separate wrong from right. You must take care of your Self. The Pure Light of God is within you.*"

Lack of Self-Love

We feel lonely, unloved, unwanted, unhappy, worried, unfulfilled and are driven by an intense desire to fill this void. Unhappiness equals non-commitment to the Self and non-acceptance of the Self. Self-love brings about inner joy, peace, compassion and the fulfillment of all desires. The Golden Angel said, "*You expect too much of yourself. Learn to love yourself, knowing that you have faults; but love yourself despite the faults. Love yourself.*"

The White Angel said, "*You are looking for the freedom of Self. You are beating your head against the wall by feeling unworthy of self-love, self-respect, self-acceptance, and happiness. It is all within, absolutely nothing is without. Take your stand, make your decision, and learn to be a little more flexible. Don't you want to experience true love in your life? Cultivate your own unconditional love by total acceptance of Self without any judgments, lacking of Self, irritations and blaming."*

Positive Affirmations of the Self

I was given the following affirmations so that I might learn self-love, and I happily share them with you:

> I am worthy of self-love and self-respect.
>
> I deserve love of the Self and self-worth.
>
> I am in total acceptance of the Self, physically, emotionally, mentally and spiritually, as well as everything I choose to do in life.
>
> I give permission to love and respect myself despite my imperfections, lack and habits. This is who I am. I have total and absolute acceptance of myself.

Self-Discipline

Self-discipline involves commitment and devotion to our Self by listening to Self and the angels – not the ego. We must commit to finding truth by knowing our Self. It is a discipline to have a conscience. In other words, we discipline our ego by not allowing it to overpower our minds when we make decisions. The list of qualities involving self-discipline is very long because it contains our stains and emotional reactions. Often as a child, I was told "Take a deep breath and count to ten before you answer or say anything." I now understand this practice. We remove the instantaneous reaction that comes from ego. We step away from ego, and, by taking a deep breath, we connect to our soul. Our focus is thereby shifted from negative to positive.

Lesson of Self-Sacrifice

I was given the following instruction on self-sacrifice: "*You sacrifice your Self by listening and following others and not your Self. You let others choose and condition your mind. You don't stand in the light of your own truth.*" The Golden Angel said, *"Sacrifice of Self is a disrespect of your Self. The Self is given away, and you become a target to be taken advantage of."*

Lesson of Loyalty

Loyalty is to be loyal to the soul, not the emotions or ego. The Blue Angel instructed: *"Loyalty is to follow the angels' teachings with total commitment, devotion, respect and gratitude. It is being honest to your feelings and being able to stand in the light of your own truth. Always speak your own truth."* At times the lessons were hard, but I needed to learn exactly what my issues were. The Blue Angel said, *"You have no faith, no trust and you don't do self questioning. You don't have total commitment, devotion, respect or gratitude. Have faith; faith means unquestionable, un-*

doubting commitment and belief in Self. Learn loyalty and trust and see the truth, use the power of self. Learn to have patience, tolerance and acceptance."

Healing the Self

I came to fully understand what the Blue Angel was teaching. I had always felt a lack of self and a lack of everything in life. I could see that my lack of self was reflected in outer conditions. Whenever I felt a lack of love, I experienced a deep void, an emptiness for which I knew not why. I knew I needed to heal my soul and recapture my Power of Self.

I prayed to the angels to cast out these negative reflections and to replace them by God's love and light. I thanked them for their wisdom and healing. At this point, I learned to distinguish between the pain of my soul and the pain of my heart. The pain that issued from my heart seemed to sit on my chest, ready to be released. My soul issues, however, seemed much deeper; it felt like they were in my upper stomach area. According to my observation and feelings, the soul appears to reside in the solar plexus area, which is right below the rib cage and above the navel. The healing of my soul continued with the healing of my heart.

Because the ego constantly betrays the Self, the soul suffers as much pain as the heart. The soul is neither free nor at peace because we often ignore its pain, needs and desire. The soul yearns for the return of God's love and light so it can recapture its Power of Self and be liberated from the bondage of ego and Maya. When we heal the Self, we free the Self. Through this journey or process, we can break free from the cycle of reincarnation or we can choose differently. This freedom occurs once we are able to work through and heal our patterns, emotional issues, stains, past-life karmic patterns and emotional issues.

I began to understand how truth lies within the Self. The Self is covered with layers of emotional issues and the seven stains. Unless the heart and Self are healed by the application of the angels' teachings, an individual cannot feel oneness with the angels and God. But there can be other methods by which one can get rid of these issues because God's creativity is unlimited.

The Blue Angel said, *"Deliverance, success, oneness, and happiness come from healing the Self, but you have a freedom of choice, either to walk the path of a balanced Self or lose the balance."*

The White Angel added: *"All of the Self will automatically be there once you learn total and absolute acceptance of the Self. Forgive, accept, release and let go to free yourself. Freedom of Self means setting the mind free from negative conditioning."*

All earthbound souls give the Power of Self to negative choices because of the negative aspect or polarity of the physical world. Positive choice and peace rest within the soul. Our soul being a part of God, longs to experience true love, peace, joy, and be free from the negative conditioning of our ego and emotions. Freedom of Self comes when the heart's issues are healed. Healing of the Self leads to oneness and wholeness with God.

The Blue Angel said, *"Everything ultimately leads to a balance. If you walk the path of balance, the angels will guide, accept and heal. The angels are teachers and healers. Mortals cannot heal or teach. Mortals are the examples of the angels at work."*

I have found that acceptance is the key to attaining oneness with God. Until I had total and absolute acceptance of my Self, I did not progress very far in learning my lessons. Acceptance and practising self-discipline are a slow process towards the last level of acceptance. As the White Angel explained: *"Acceptance is a given factor and if you cannot accept yourself, you cannot accept our teachings. Like your Self and know your Self."*

Acceptance will occur if we accept our stains and the emotional reactions presented in a lesson. If we cannot accept it, we cannot change it. Understanding can only be there if we analyze the experiences by questioning ourselves. We must seek inner answers by listening to our heart. Ask the angels for an understanding of the experience. This is homework on our Self that we all must do. When we do our part, the angels provide.

The Blue Angel said, *"While learning from us, an individual soul requires acceptance, patience, discipline, trust and faith to follow their heart's feelings. Listen deeply, have faith, trust and understanding. Without these, you will not move anywhere. Trust in yourself, in the teachings and in your instincts. Feel it, know it, and act upon it. Decisions lead to discoveries."*

Our lives are filled with spiritual teachings and lessons. The essence of life is in the individual experience. The experiences of my journey are used to demonstrate the application of the angels' teachings and how to apply this philosophy in daily life. We must all learn individually about our Self from our own experiences.

Sometimes it is difficult to recognize our own issues and habits because we are accustomed to them. Not only are we accustomed to them, but it also takes great time and analysis to connect the present situation to a childhood incident or parental, handed-down conditions. There are many emotions involved in one incident. For me, I need to look at the emotions I am feeling in the present. I then return to the past to search for the same childhood emotions. I believe my current pain to be a result of past issues. If we can accept and feel this as truth, we resolve and heal our present issues.

I knew my healing process was not yet finished, but I had no idea what issues remained. In March 2004, I was given further insight into my soul's karmic patterns (past-life trauma of death and blueprints). My soul carried these patterns into the present lifetime to be experienced, endured, resolved and healed on its last levels. I knew this process of healing would free my soul from the cycle of repeating the issue in another life time. I had already been told about a centuries old, Egyptian past-life and how I was put to death (beheaded).

Throughout my life I suffered greatly from throat infections. They always worsened, and medication only brought minor relief. My family members always recovered on their own. While rewriting this chapter, my throat once again became badly infected. I felt weak, extremely hungry and thirsty. I could not understand why I felt so hungry and thirsty. My daughter agreed: "Usually we lose our appetite when we are sick like this."

To rewrite this chapter, I re-read my 1995 journal[13] to see if I had missed anything. I re-read the detailed description of my death in a past-life. I had a sore throat at the time, and I must have asked the Angel for an explanation because the Angel said: *"Rekha must seal and heal her throat."* I did the steps of healing described in the process and procedure for healing, and I was okay.

I must admit that at that time I had no self-trust and did not completely believe the revelation about my past life. Nine years later, I found it very difficult to endure this experience, but I now understood. I understood why I was hungry and thirsty because I was kept without food and drink before I was put to

13 God and the angels gave me these teachings at that time

death (beheaded). I also knew what the angels required of me. With this healing, I was amazed to find that I was healed from another physical ailment. I discovered that my long-existing shoulder pain had almost gone. A week later, it disappeared completely. I had had this pain for many years. I underwent massage and acupuncture a year previously, but the pain remained. As more issues related to this past-life show up, I heal them. I clearly recall the words of the Creator: "*When you seek, and as you seek, all will be revealed to you.*"

The Angels' Purpose in Teaching

The angels teach through our thought-forms; their purpose is the ultimate salvation and freedom of all souls. We constantly receive guidance from the angels through our thought-forms or in a symbolic form in physical experiences when we seek answers. This symbolic guidance through physical experiences is hard to recognize, and takes time, but we understand once we become accustomed to the angels' teachings.

This book is intended as a tool to apply angelic teachings and philosophies in our present lives so we may discover our issues and patterns. The angels make their teaching available to all souls who are ready to embark upon this journey.

It cannot be stated too often that everything in life has a purpose, meaning and lessons. If we embrace this point of view and seek the answers, we will discover that there is neither good nor bad, only learning. Of course, something good can always come out of a difficult experience if we learn our lesson from it. Good or bad is labelled by human emotions. Our purpose on this planet is to learn, to heal and to free our Selves.

Angelic teachings, while simple in nature, are often difficult to put into practice. Human emotion and stains cloud our judgment and often cause us to make negative choices. Ultimately these choices lead to lessons. Bear in mind the wisdom of the Creator: *"Every event is planned for the Soul's journey; one cannot blame others or themselves for it."*

How to Embark upon a Healing Journey with the Angels

Start and end your day with the prayer written in Chapter Two. If you need to pray more frequently, then do so. Write about your dreams and experiences in a daily journal. Analyze these incidents. Find the symbolic connection between your issues, patterns and stains, and what is taking place in your present situation and discover its connection to parental issues.

Write down the incidents that are bothering you. Analyze your own emotional behaviours, patterns, reactions and conversations that take place. Pay attention to your ego and anger so you can figure out how and why the situation is hurting you. This becomes your homework on your Self. Practice self-discipline by keeping your attention on your Self and not blaming, judging, criticizing or finding fault with others. This is the only way you will accept your own faults.

Mentally revisit your childhood and start looking for the same pattern, issue or parental, handed-down habits, situations and pain. Accept that you are angry and that your ego is not allowing you to accept your shortcomings. Once you recognize the childhood incident that is re-creating the same issues in the here and now, it will be easier to accept your ego, anger, behaviour, patterns, reactions, etc. Realize that it is *your* problem. *You* are attracting these situations repeatedly and re-opening old wounds and issues.

Once you accept your shortcomings, it is easier to forgive yourself for suffering the hardship created by these issues. Only then can you forgive others and forgive those who have participated in re-opening your wounds. Heal the inner child's wounded heart with the steps described in the process and procedures of healing.

Example of Parental, Handed-Down Issues

A friend and I keep in touch by calling one another every three or four months. Once when I spoke with her, I inquired about her well-being. She replied that she was working seven days a week and struggling to make ends meet. She explained that her situation had been like this for many years, and she feared the stress might cause a mental breakdown.

She was helping a daughter who had returned to live with her; her life and living arrangement felt very cluttered. I asked if these were the conditions her parents lived under while she was growing up. She said yes. I asked if she wanted to be free from these issues. She willingly accepted my help, and I guided her step-by-step through the process of healing. I advised her to continue to pray for healing of her inner child until the issue was resolved.

I called her the next day because I knew there would be more issues that she might not recognize. When I asked how she was feeling, she responded that she was feeling lighter and better but very tired. She told me that since the previous summer, she had been looking for a house outside of Ottawa. When I replied, "As if you have time for this!" She said, "Well, I have to run around to fill the void."

I then asked if this was the way her mother worked – to the point of exhaustion – and if she was always running away from her parents' house. She said, "This is so true! I am reliving my parents actions and my childhood." I said to her, "You are running away from your Self. You can do the healing on these issues and will not have a need to find a house – instead you will find your soul and peace within." She agreed to work on these issues. Her healing journey with the angels continues as it was written in her Book of Life.

In another example, a client of mine told me that she was trying to get her roommate to take responsibility for his actions. When I asked if he reminded her of anyone from her childhood, she responded, "My father". I told her that she could heal the issue with the angels' help, and release and let go of her father by accepting him the way he was. We went through the process of healing: to heal and release the little girl from this issue. She felt the presence of an angel during this session.

Example of a Childhood Issue

Another friend of mine said that she had just this one issue with her large dog. When she walks him and he sees another dog, he suddenly takes off. The swift jerking on the leash causes her back pain, and she is afraid of this. I asked her to look at the emotional trauma stemming from this situation and try to connect it to a childhood issue. I also asked that she try to discover who caused it in the first place – the dog was simply a vehicle for re-opening old issues. She realized that this was an issue with her father. We did the process of healing. She reported improved behaviour on the part of her dog and less back pain.

If you recognize any awakening, thanks and gratitude belong to the angels.
Thank you, angels, for the knowledge and wisdom you provide to us mortals.

Lessons in Learning on Various Topics

Please protect, bless and cleanse this chapter. Thank you.

Freedom of Choice

THE BLUE ANGEL SAID, *"Destiny, fate and purpose in life depend upon the individual's freedom of choice."*

As our individual soul makes its choices, the angels provide and write its destiny accordingly. The angels know all about us and the choices we are going to make. Everything is prewritten and predestined. In other words, we are responsible for making our choices, and in turn we are responsible for our fate, destiny and life purpose. Our ego (stains) and emotional issues can influence our choices and divert us from the path of knowing our Self.

Freedom of choice is a given right for all souls. One can

choose success and happiness in the material world or success and happiness in God's world. Eventually, we have to give up one choice for the sake of the other. We cannot have both. This becomes clearer with experience – experiences presented as lessons. Material success cannot buy true happiness, nor can it provide love for Self, health or inner peace.

The Golden Angel said, *"There are many choices and many lessons to be learned. Only a few can comprehend the meaning of freedom of choice."*

This made me realize that when making decisions through the scope of stains and emotional need, we have many desires and many choices. When we make decisions based on the soul's need, we have one choice and one desire: to know our Self and to know God. There really are only two choices: either we allow our ego to lead us, complete with its stains and emotions and foundation in the material world and Maya, or we choose to know our Self and make decisions based on Divine truth. This does not mean that we cannot earn a living honestly and with integrity. Know that we are exactly where we are meant to be and are doing precisely what we are supposed to do. It is all destined so that we learn. The White Angel explained: *"When you learn what you have to learn, then you will not be comfortable with what you are doing. That will be the time to do something else in life."*

I have always felt a great need for answers in my life because deep within I have felt empty, alone and unhappy. Often, I wondered what I was searching for and what I really wanted from life. I now realize that I am left with one choice, but I have been given the freedom to choose. I made a conscious decision to follow the angels' teachings, no matter what my life experience would be. Actually, this decision was made a long time ago; in fact, ever since I began searching. Once my angelic instruction began, I found it was not so difficult to re-enforce this decision.

The Blue Angel reminded me: *"Ultimately all choices are ours."*

As a matter of fact, I realized that an individual soul has no further choices to make once he or she makes a conscious decision to follow divine teachings. We accept our lessons in knowing our Self so that we may find that inner peace that we all desire. Once the soul becomes one with the angels and God, it will automatically follow God's will.

Life constantly gives me what I need to learn. I have learned to accept life's terms to accomplish that end. This decision leads me to the discovery of Self, the truth of self, freedom of self, and a blessed oneness with the angels and God. I finally understand that destiny, fate and purpose begin with freedom of choice. When we make a conscious decision to know our Self, we arrive at God's plan for us. Oneness with all.

Fear

The Blue Angel spoke of fear: *"Fear is a conflict of emotions. There is no place for fear among men [people]. Fear is negative and obsessive. The only thing you have to fear is fear itself."* The balance of fear is love for Self, self-belief, self-trust and faith in Self, the angels and God.

I created an issue of fear when I gave my power of Self to negative choices in my childhood. I had a feeling that fear came first, then my ego took over. I was extremely frightened of being alone in the forest. My fear continued to manifest in different circumstances throughout my life. I was afraid of the Blue Angel. My fear surfaced in his presence. He was very tall, spoke in a thundering voice and told me that I was hiding behind my emotions: "*Why are you afraid, and what are you afraid of?*"

I realized that it was fear of the negative choices I had made in my childhood. By not listening and walking away from my childhood experiences with the angel, I suffered. I prayed for forgiveness and asked, "Please help me so that I will never wander from this path again." I was afraid of abandonment, being left alone and being left to find my own way. I needed to endure this experience again in order to release my fear on its last level; only then could emotional healing occur. As I wrestled with fear, it often left me feeling suffocated, unable to breathe and sleep. It was a crippling state, perhaps much akin to anxiety attacks. After I had prayed about these issues in this life time and in my past lives, I was told by the angel that I had abandoned the book of truth that I had written in a previous life because of doubt and fear. I had allowed fear and doubt to overtake me. My issues disappeared, but not before I once again physically endured them in my present life.

My fear was created by a lack of self-trust, self-belief, and faith in Self. As soon as I doubted, fear set in; my power of Self was immediately taken over by my ego. My ego only allowed me to look for help outside of myself. I felt powerless in the situation and often wanted to give up and die. As different situations caused overwhelming emotions to overtake me, I often felt this way. The Angel firmly and lovingly stated: "*Dying is not an option; it is an easy way out instead of learning.*"

My childhood experience of being lost in the forest deeply

scarred my psyche. I blamed myself and saw my fear as weakness. I told myself that if I had had enough faith in myself, I would have prayed to God to find my way out of the forest. As I learned, I discovered that action not only takes trust in Self but also courage and self-determination. I have also learned that when doubt creeps in, I must use common sense – a faculty of soul or a creative aspect of soul – to examine the situation. When I do this, fear immediately dissipates and doubts disappear. Decisions always lead to discovery. I also realized that our worries and concerns are derived from our fears. When there is no fear, there are no worries and concerns. It is all positive and good.

Other Examples of Fear

A client came to my house and saw my budgies sitting on top of their cage. She froze in fear, asking me if they were going to fly at her. I locked the birds in the cage and asked her, "What happened to you with birds in your childhood?"

She explained that her sister used to chase her with a toy bird, making loud bird sounds, and she would run, screaming in fear. I asked her if she wanted to face her fear and get rid of it. She said yes. I prayed to the angels to bring her back to her childhood and bubble everyone. Then I asked her, "What do you see?" She told me that she was running and screaming because her sister was chasing her with the bird. I said, "Stop running. Turn around to talk to your sister, and look directly into her eyes."

As soon as she did that, her sister froze in her tracks. Four very tall, pink angels, two on each side of her, appeared. They held her hand and brought her close to her sister. I told her to tell her sister, through the little girl (herself as a child), that she no longer wanted to be afraid of birds. She needed to give this fear and pursuit back to her sister, with the help of the angels, and thank her. I then said the rest of the prayer for healing and cleansing. We thanked the angels and God. Healing was received to a level where she felt comfortable to sit in the same room with the birds without rapid palpitations. Not everyone sees the angels: some feel a presence, or peace, or lightness or perhaps nothing – regardless, healing is provided at its earned level.

Another friend, and co-worker, had a fear of driving and did not have a driver's licence. When I inquired about a childhood incident, she told me that her father had once fallen asleep while driving. She was terrified by a fast approaching car that was directly in their path. She woke her father just in time to avoid an accident. We asked for healing from the angels. Now, two years later, she has her driving licence. Prior to taking her driving test, she revisited the place where this incident took place to complete her healing.

Mirror Reflections

We are the mirror reflection of our parents. In other words, we reflect our parents' emotional issues and habits. Sometimes we even have their patterns incorporated into our own behaviours and act them out consciously or unconsciously. Similarly, our children are mirror reflections of our emotional imbalances, habits, attitudes, stains, patterns, etc. Today's children have more freedom to express their anger without fear; as a result, they may behave aggressively towards us so that we can recognize our shortcomings. My lesson was presented to me in this manner so I could take a good look at myself and learn to change instead of blaming my child.

This does not mean that the child's behaviour is appropriate. Once we learn this, only then can we teach the child. Remember if we are on a learning journey with the angels to learn about our Self, then focus must remain on the Self – all else is judgment. This lesson was presented to me when I asked the angels, "Why is my son giving me such a hard time?" The Angel replied, *"There is a mirror in every household. Your son is not hard; he is walking in his father's shoes."*

As I considered this response, I realized it to be true. All this time I had been blaming and judging my son. As I examined and analyzed my emotions, I found that my inner child's pain and feelings of helplessness kept attracting its reflection from different souls. The play remained the same – only the acts were altered. The lessons were always the same; the method of presentation varied.

We attract souls in our professional, personal or romantic relationships because our mirror reflections re-open each other's old wounds so that healing may occur. Unless we commit to learning these lesson, we become argumentative, angry, blaming and judgmental. Often in partnerships or marriage, we walk away from one another without learning our lesson. Sometimes one spouse learns while the other remains totally unaware and seemingly oblivious to transformation or change. It is not ours to judge. An individual has freedom of choice and thereby chooses to learn or remain the same. If we choose not to learn, however, we will continue to attract souls who will repeat the same issues and lessons. Lessons repeat themselves until they are learned and healed. Keep in mind, it is not necessarily our spouse or relationship that presents our lesson, it can be presented by any soul around us. Lessons come in many ways, such as the death of loved ones or other occurrences.

Personal Lessons

The Blue Angel said, *"Make no compromises with worldly ties of friendship, relatives, family and others when it comes to your spiritual values and following the angels' teachings."*

Spiritual values must not be compromised. I learned this lesson clearly and firmly from the angels when I almost compromised my ethics by helping a friend. In 1995, my friend's husband asked if he could park his car in my driveway for a few days. He was trying to hide from people involved in a messy legal dispute. He was a high-pressure salesman who was being sued by a customer. Without thinking I was doing anything wrong, I agreed to let him use my driveway. I did not realize that I should not be a part of this unethically created, negative situation. The angels were unhappy because I did not stand up for my truth. The Blue Angel asked me, *"Where is your conscience? Who are you? You are fighting with your conscience. You gave away your conscience by sheltering your friend from his karmic consequences. One little slip and you have spoiled it all."*

Because of my lack of Self, I seemed to be doing everything wrong at that time. The angels knew everything about my worries and fears: I was having financial worries at the time. The Blue Angel said, *"Why has such importance been placed on tokens? You do not follow the teachings and select the ones that fit the moment by picking and choosing. You are not standing in the light of your own truth. Your lack of faith, trust, and belief in Self and God is holding you back from speaking your truth. Where is your undoubting commitment and belief in the angels and the Creator? There should be absolutely no compromise for spiritual values and truth with any of your family, friends, relatives and others."*

The Blue Angel continued: *"Never compromise your value of truth. You change your perspective, you lose balance, and if you lose your balance, you have lost everything. Do not sell yourself short. If you don't put a value and respect on your self, you don't value the teachings."* The White Angel added: *"Use kindness, understanding, acceptance, and honesty in speaking your truth, and never compromise that. Be prudent and predicated to speak about your truth."*

I apologized for my ignorance and asked forgiveness. I then apologized to my friend and told him I could not be involved in a situation that affected his own karmic consequences. As you can see, the angels became involved in all aspects of my life. Situations like this made me aware of their complete knowledge and ongoing love and instruction. This is but one of many lessons I have learned with the angels' guidance.

At one point I felt empty – as if I were making little progress. I began reading spiritual material hoping to find relief. The library books gave me a headache, and I felt like I was doing something wrong. The Blue Angel said, *"By reading other books you are establishing someone else's thought-forms. None of your thought-forms are left."*

I learned from this experience that I was avoiding inner searching. The books were simply a form of procrastination because I was not ready to focus entirely on my Self. As I looked outside of my Self for answers, I lost my balance and overlooked the opportunity to find the necessary answers within. Once again, I lacked trust in Self and I looked to an outside source: in this instance, books. The Angel said, *"Until you have freedom of Self, you must be committed to the Self."*

This is not to be misunderstood. Spiritual books have their value, and reading is often very therapeutic for many, but when you are on a spiritual journey – a quest for Self healing, you must do the inner work. You can read other spiritual books as long as the ideas or ideologies you are reading are taken as guidelines and do not disrupt your focus on your Self. Information provides guidelines; it does not give answers. Answers come from within. (You are not on *their* journey; you are on *your own*, very personal, spiritual journey.)

In a similar situation when I was searching for inner peace and contentment, I decided to find a job to rid myself of boredom. Feeling unmotivated and depressed, I thought that a job would keep my mind occupied. I would not have as much time to pay attention to my feelings of lack of Self or my inner void. Once again, the angels provided direct and loving insight: *"You want to depend on something outer to give you a boost to do something. If you can't clean up what is going on inside of you, how can a job provide what you need?"* This was during a period in my life when the angels created circumstances that forced me to work on my emotional issues and patterns. If I had run away from these feelings, I would missed an opportunity to learn. Once my issues were resolved and understood at a particular level, I began working.

As the angels continued to teach me, unknowingly I tried to help others before I was ready. I was taught yet another lesson. I began sharing the teachings with family, friends and others before learning and absorbing them myself. I found myself completely drained and depleted of energy. When I questioned the angels about these feelings, I was told: *"You have no self-confidence and confidentiality towards the teachings. When sharing them with others, you have not given yourself a chance to absorb them completely. All of these teachings have been* **your** *lesson, not for your family or others. The more you share them, the weaker the link becomes [with the angels' energy]. You gave them [the teachings] all away too soon, before you had a chance to absorb them. Therefore, you haven't learned anything. You are chasing your own tail, going in circles, getting nowhere, and in the process losing all your energy."*

I realized that knowing the truth is only half the knowledge. Without practice and absorption of the lessons, there is no full realization. I was also unaware that the knowledge was personally mine and not meant to be shared. After this realization, I kept the teachings to myself. Angelic teachings are individual and personal. They are given in confidentiality and trust. They cannot be shared until an individual soul has achieved freedom of Self. There will always be certain teachings that cannot be shared until they are learned and earned because we are constantly learning and growing spiritually.

In the beginning, when the angels began to present their teachings, I had a hard time believing that they were really teaching me and that this was actually happening to *me*. One part of me (my soul) would believe, but the other part (ego) would leave me in total disbelief. My ego would not allow me to listen to the angels when they asked me to throw away all the spiritual material I had accumulated over the years. It took me awhile before I disposed of all the material. The angels knew that I was having a problem believing in them and that I was still reading the old spiritual materials.

The Blue Angel demonstrated his strength by manifesting it on the physical level and said, *"You don't believe in us and in our teachings. This will show you to believe in us."* The Blue Angel, in its physical form, appears very tall, with a muscular body and is always in a flowing motion. The face is difficult to see because of the brilliancy of his light. He is presented as a protector because he is the guardian angel for all souls.

The Blue Angel used my friend's arms to show his strength on the physical level. My friend had come to visit and we were sitting on folding lawn chairs with plastic armrests. We were simply discussing our spiritual journeys and matters that we felt required further work. All of a sudden, the Blue Angel came through and spoke the above words. As he was saying "This will show you to believe in us," my friends hands slightly pressed on the arm rest, and they instantly snapped. The chair began to fold, and my friend started to fall with it. I quickly arose to catch her before she fell to the floor. We both were shocked but knew it all to be true and good. This experience had a powerful impact. After that, I neither doubted nor disbelieved what the angels told me. They were never wrong; everything I was ever told, happened.

We must accept and follow exactly what they say. There is a reason for everything the angels are teaching. After this experience, I disposed of all my old spiritual material. It has been nine years since then, and now I can read what I want to because it no longer affects my thought-forms.

I have also encountered the Blue Angel as a German Shepherd that appeared out of nowhere during my early morning walks. This was an unusually tall and big dog. The first words that came out of my mouth were, "Oh my, where have you come from?" He was gentle and playful with me. I stayed for a while but then left because I was afraid to be alone with such a large dog. As I was walked away, the angel told me, in my thought-forms, that I had met an angel! I looked back, and there was nothing. This particular breed of dog also symbolizes a protector of man with great strength. Later, I asked why I had met an angel in a physical form. The angel said, *"To give you strength with your journey."* I thanked the angels for watching over my soul throughout my life.

I also felt the Blue Angel's might in his thundering, rolling voice when he asked: *"Where is your conscience? Who are you? One little slip and you have spoiled it all."* It felt like the whole universe was shaking. The Blue Angel knows what it takes to teach a human soul. It leaves a permanent effect because the teachings are absorbed and experienced by the soul. The angels are powerful and mighty. One can feel their power, yet they are the most gentle and humble beings.

At one point during our teaching, the angels took us to meet souls who had once walked on earth and had attained balance and wholeness: they had become one with the angels and God in a circle of divine light. The Creator, angels and all of these souls were present. We were told that it was not important to know the names of these souls. One of them came forward to give me the teachings. We immediately recognized him; we knew he was Jesus. He carried the pure, brilliant, golden light of God and had a sacred heart with golden light shining through it. We walked with him and bathed in the Creator's golden divine light, which cleansed our heart, mind and soul. We felt at peace.

Jesus said: *"Live with faith and prayers, healing and balance. Always speak your truth. Always stand in the light of your truth. Take my staff*[14] *and go to the mountain and speak the word of God. When you speak, the Creator will come through you. Trust, affirm, be sincere and believe. You will become one with the angels and God. Be strong and speak your truth; you are not alone."*

Dreams

Dreams are a very important part of the angels' teachings. Through our dreams, the angels often tell us the answers to our questions or prepare us for what is taking place or about to take place in our lives. My lessons of stains and emotional issues were often repeatedly presented in my dreams. Most dreams are given in a symbolic form, which often makes them difficult to understand. Repeated dreams should be the ones you make the most effort to understand. According to my understanding, dreams can be categorized in three different aspects of learning:

1. Straightforward dreams
2. Symbolic dreams and
3. Confusing dreams involving fear.

Straightforward dreams can be given as situations of the past, present or future. Past dreams could be of past lives. Dreams of the present simply show the present issue of our habit or stain such as ego, anger, lust, attachment, greed, hatred or jealousy.

14 Editor's comment: this imagery is synonymous with 'the Good Shepherd" of the New Testament. He carries a staff or walking stick

The future is shown either in a symbolic manner or simply as a prediction of what will take place.

Symbolic dreams are more common and more difficult to interpret. These dreams are usually connected to our present emotional conditions, issues and feelings. Recurring dreams should be paid attention to because they are important lessons that the angels want us to learn. To analyze symbolic dreams, we have to ask questions like "What does this thing, person or animal symbolize according to my knowledge or understanding?" Death may symbolize a loss or a new beginning. For instance, in one of my dreams, I saw a beautiful, happy little girl playing, then moments later she drowned in a pool. I watched her drown but did nothing to save her. This dream symbolized my emotional state: I was drowning in my emotions and doing nothing to save my Self." The little girl symbolized my soul.

One of my recurring dreams was that I was totally unprepared for a final exam that I was scheduled to write the following day. I felt fearful and anxious in trying to decide whether to write the exam or not. After two or three such dreams, I realized that I had to work on the little girl's fear. I prayed for her healing on the last level, but the dream returned. In the last dream, I was prepared and knew my material well. I could answer the questions, but I wanted to review my textbook. I had misplaced the book and could not find it anywhere. This time I decided to pray to the Angel of Knowledge to provide an answer to this dream. The Angel asked, *"What does the exam and book symbolize?"* I realized the answer immediately although I had never thought of it in this manner before. I said the exam is the final test of my faith in the book, *Emotional Healing with the Angels*. I realized that the angels had tested me in my dreams many times, for this particular lesson, and finally it has been learned. I then told the Angel that I have total faith, trust and belief in myself and in the book; I gave the angels' book back to them. I thanked them for the dream, its meaning and the lesson. The dream never returned.

Confusing dreams, where too many changes are taking place, represent our present state of mind. In this state, negativity takes over. Fear is not always present in these dreams although it can be. If fear is present, it is usually the issue for which we are being tested. One of my recurring, fearful dreams involved being chased by a lion. As I ran for my life, sometimes I escaped and other times I was killed. These dreams were terrifying. In my final dream I turned around, stood still and faced the lion. He transformed into a little girl. The lion was the little girl's fear, which meant that it was my own fear and I was running away from it. I recalled the angel's words: *"The only thing you have to fear is fear itself."*

Negative dreams can be cast away by prayer: use all three parts of the prayer for healing as soon as you wake up. This cleanses your heart, mind, body, thought-forms and spirit and also begins your day with positive energy.

Thought-Forms

During the spiritual journey, our thought-forms are a very important part of learning. We must learn to distinguish between when they are simply our thoughts and when they are inspired by the angels. All negative thought-forms are ours, which come from our stains and emotional imbalances. Also, if you have been asking a question for quite some time and the answer suddenly shows up in your thought-form, you can be sure this is coming from the angels. Acknowledge where it came from and give thanks accordingly. In a balanced state, all thought-forms become pure. In this state, there is no difference in our thinking or God's thinking.

The Creator said, *"When you seek, and as you seek and ask, all will be revealed to you. Seek the pure thought-forms for everyone by getting a blue light. These thought-forms are no longer your attachments but your responsibility to Self. Respect the balance."*

Physical Healings

This anecdote is about the instant healing of physical pain I have been blessed to receive. Any soul can be similarly blessed if they ask and pray. The first miraculous healing occurred in my childhood in Kashmir. Our family was crossing a snow-covered, mountain valley on horseback. It was about a two- to three-hour journey. Within ten to fifteen minutes into our journey, a terrific snowstorm descended upon us. It was freezing cold, and I discovered that I had only one glove. I tried to keep my bare hand in my pocket, but soon my gloved hand was freezing also. The wind was blowing hard, and there was poor visibility. My father gave me a handkerchief to wrap around my bare hand, but it did not help.

Soon my hands were frozen and numb. I started crying in pain. I cried all the way to our destination to seek shelter. I knew my hands were frostbitten, but they had warmed in no time. When my father looked at my hands, they were perfectly normal. Everyone was surprised, but I knew deep inside that God must have heard my cries for help. I did not know then that the angels had protected my hands from freezing and healed them.

The second incident that I remember occurred in 1992. I was scheduled for minor surgery. Someone told me about the terrible pain that I would experience after surgery. I became concerned, but it was too late to cancel. While I was in the hospital awaiting surgery, I began to pray. I prayed hard for healing, not knowing if my prayers would be heard. When I awoke from the surgery, I felt no pain. I was released within a few hours. I thought that the pain would start sooner or later, but I experienced no pain at all. I rested for one day, and within a week I was completely healed and able to go back to work.

This gave me trust, faith and belief in the power of prayer and in divine healing. Prayers are always answered if we pray without expectation. I realized that an innocent child's cries in a helpless situation are also heard as prayer. I thanked the angels for always healing souls in need.

In 1997, I worked from my apartment in Florida as an esthetician and massage therapist. A girl from the next building, who was sent by a friend, came to see me for a back massage. I was unaware of this girl's pain or condition. While I worked her back, she told me that her lower back hurt a lot. I asked her if she believed in the angels. She said, "Yes." I asked her if she wanted me to pray for her pain. She said, "Yes." As I massaged her back, I simply said all three parts of the prayer for healing. I then asked her to thank the angels and God. She did. After the massage she felt so good, she wanted to return every week. I did not see her professionally again.

Three or four months later, I saw her at the pool. She said,

"Hi, Rekha, do you know what happened that day when you gave me a massage?" I said, "No." She said, "When I came to see you, I was in very bad shape with lower back pain and was ready to go for surgery. My father had surgery for the same problem. The pain was so bad that I could not get up to go to the bathroom without someone's help. But after the massage that night, I found myself sitting on the toilet wondering how I got there. Within a week or so, my pain was completely gone. Look, I can bend now, and I am taking a course to become a massage therapist." I was very happy for her.

This only happens when a soul has learned the lesson through endurance and earned healing in the angels' time.

Lesson of Helping Other Souls

My lesson of helping other souls was given by the White Angel. I was asked if I was here to save and help other souls. I thought I might be able to help but certainly not save. The angel already picked up my answer through my thought-forms before I could respond. Then the Angel of Salvation and Redemption, who carries a huge white cross filled with brilliant, pure white light, handed his cross to me, saying, *"If you want to help and save souls then take the responsibility for it."*

The cross was so big and heavy that I could not carry its weight. I could not even take a single step, let alone walk with it. I realized that I had made a mistake, so I apologized to the White Angel. I now understood that I am here only to learn about my Self. I cannot possibly save others because every journey is individual. Every soul must take this journey on his or her own. With this answer, the White Angel with Golden Eyes, who lights the path for souls to follow their salvation, took back his cross and released me. I thanked the angels for my lesson and for their wisdom. I was taught when humans help another humans to recognize their Higher Self, they becomes an example of angels at work.

After finishing writing and reviewing this book, one morning during my daily walks, I said to God, "Now that I have fulfilled your will by writing this book on your behalf, what will I be doing next?" I heard the reply "From now on your will and desires will be fulfilled." I thought *my will!* Then I started to examine my wishes and desires and found one of them was that many souls achieve enlightenment of the Self by knowing that all paths eventually leads to balanced state of consciousness. Then I came to the conclusion that since I am one with God and angels in a Circle of Divine Light, my will and God's will are in alignment or the same. I thanked God with a big smile. My heart and soul are filled with joy, peace and divine love forever.

My journey of experiencing and expanding in Self continues with God and the angels. I also realized that the Blue Angel is God himself who has taught me and continues to teach me. God can take any form or shape to teach a human soul.

God bless all souls.
Thank you.

With this we thank the Creator and the angels for teaching us mortals to walk in the light of our own truth. We request protection, blessings and cleansing for the entire journey through this book. We release the book in the care of the Divine Light of the Creator.

About the Author

Rekha Vidyarthi was born in India but came to Canada in 1972 from East Africa. She is an esthetician by profession. For the past fifteen years, she has been deeply involved with spirituality and has been searching for her life's purpose and the meaning of her childhood experiences with God and the angels.

In 1994, angels reappeared in her life and gave her the answers through their teachings in philosophy and spiritual wisdom. She was asked to record these teachings in a book on their behalf because this was an uncompleted task from a past life.

Rekha is married, has two children, and currently lives in Florida.

Email

angels.healing@yahoo.com

(If you have any questions about your personal issues,
I may direct you where to look for the answer and heal.)

www.ingramcontent.com/pod-product-compliance
Ingram Content Group UK Ltd.
Pitfield, Milton Keynes, MK11 3LW, UK
UKHW041942190726
13854UKWH00004B/1737